Workplace buzz on Anna's concepts and seminars:

I participated in her seminar with my entire staff. You won't be the same after hearing what Anna has to share—even years later.

—Heidi Hudson-Roberts, HickoryTech Sales Support Supervisor

Anna has been instrumental in building trust within our executive team and throughout the organization. We use her ideas on a daily basis.

—Rob Tracey, COO, Intek Plastics

I've kept the materials in the top drawer of my desk for seven years.

—Graham Holden, CEO, Marshalls, England

This family business runs lean and mean with a tight group of intelligent and energetic leaders. Before working with Anna, our relationships and communication techniques were in pressing need of a tune-up. Anna moved us from a culture that was frequently dominated by conflict, to a positive climate of support—part of our formula for success!

—Richard Murphy, CEO, Murphy Warehouse

My stress level has plummeted!

—Dan Janal, President, PR Leads

Attending this seminar was the best money we've ever spent.

—Paul Jennings, QA, Rolls Royce, England

I use her materials every day.

—Greg Lee, CEO, Carl Zeiss, IMT

Brilliant, witty, engaging.

—Terry Weight, Shell Oil, Netherlands

Unless you live on a deserted island and never have to deal with people, you need to see this presentation. I'm a better person and we're a better organization.

—Sam Richter, President, James J. Hill Business Library

Every corporate boardroom should have access to Anna's work. The ideas are groundbreaking and compelling, and she delivers her message with humor and depth.

—Mary Tribble, President, Tribble Creative Group, Co-Founder, Forum for Corporate Conscience

This was the best staff development presentation ever!

—Don Supalla, President, Rochester CT College

This seminar knocked my socks off—it is the next frontier of productivity.

—Rod Sando, Executive Director, Columbia Basin Fish and Wildlife Association

I have used the tools continually for the last two years and they are incredible. They have helped many people—at work and in my personal life.

—John Michael Lerma, Supervisor, AT&T Broadband

The first time I heard this seminar I felt cheated. I wished I had heard it 30 years ago.

—Larry Gigliotti, South Dakota Game, Fish and Parks

On a scale of 1 to 5 I'd rate this a 10. Union leadership and employees benefit from these ideas.

—Scott Clothier, President, International Brotherhood of Electrical Workers, Local 2047

I don't know where I'd be today as a manager if I had not learned these concepts.

—David Wehde, Clean Water Action

One of the most highly rated and appreciated seminars we've ever offered.

—Mike Hageman, CEO, J&B Group

How to
Reduce
Workplace
Conflict
and
Stress

How Leaders and Their Employees
Can Protect Their Sanity and Productivity
From Tension and Turf Wars

By

ANNA MARAVELAS

CAREER
PRESS
Pompton Plains, NJ

HOW TO REDUCE WORKPLACE CONFLICT AND STRESS
EDITED BY CHRIS CAROLEI
TYPESET BY EILEEN DOW MUNSON
Cover design by Dorothy Wachtenheim
Author photo courtesy of Tomi O'Brien
Printed in the U.S.A.

Names and locations have been changed to protect individual's privacy.

To order this title, please call toll-free 1-800-CAREER-1 (NJ and Canada: 201-848-0310) to order using VISA or MasterCard, or for further information on books from Career Press.

CAREER
PRESS

The Career Press, Inc., 220 West Parkway, Unit 12
Pompton Plains, NJ 07444
www.careerpress.com
www.newpagebooks.com

Library of Congress Cataloging-in-Publication Data

Maravelas, Anna.
    How to reduce workplace conflict and stress : how leaders and their employees can protect their sanity and productivity from tension and turf wars / by Anna Maravelas.
        p. c.m.
    Includes index.
    ISBN 1-56414-818-1 (paper)
    1. Conflict management. 2. Meditation. 3. Negotiation. 4. Interpersonal conflict. 5. Organizational behavior. 6. Teams in the workplace. I. Title.

HD42.M375 2005
658.1'053—dc22

                                        2005051322

This book is dedicated to—

My son, Benjamin,
for his wisdom and wit.

My teacher, Marie Burgeson,
for leading me to the light.

The Julie and Michael Weisser family,
Nelson Mandela,
and the people of Tibet,
for living the power of loving kindness.

Acknowledgments

M y grandmothers, Antigone and Vasiliki, who relinquished their love for Greece so that that their children might prosper; my parents, Louis and Anastasia, who remained true to their dream; Drs. Patricia and Drea Zigarmi, for decades of love and support; Margaret, Carol, and Bob Larrington, for sharing a writing haven overlooking the corn; the staff of Dwelling in the Woods and the Naniboujou Lodge and their spirit-filled retreats.

My agent, Ed Knappman, of New England Publishing Associates, for his patience and sage advice; my brother, Paul Maravelas, who skillfully edited the first draft; Karen Engelsen, for her staggering literary skills and irreverence; Nancy Clemens, for her witty poems and prose; the graphic talents of Mary Lysne, Eric at HolmDigital.com, and the Sketch Pad; Laurie Dunn, for her significant research abilities; Jim Stein for countless hours of unbilled advice; Rob Tracy, Mike Bates, John Shade, and Mark Morgan, for sharing their expertise and feedback; AJ Myers and Brian Taylor, for their skill and creativity at Web design.

Karen Borre, who put three copies of the first draft in a vault; Rod Sando and Brian Stenquist, who realized the power of these ideas, and invited me to Alaska; Terry Weight and Alan Winlow, who sponsored me at British Deming Association Conference on multiple occasions; the Mauve Weight, Jon Norrie, and Lynn Parsley families, who opened their homes and hearts; Judy and Virgil Vinz and their countless acts of neighborly love.

My outrageous Greek family, siblings, aunties, nieces, and cousins, including my "adopted" sister, Magda, and treasured friends Fran VanBockel, Mary Butler, Margaret Kloster, Charlotte Mardell, Bob Howell, Pam Sheldon, David Barrymore, Maggie Capocasa, Greg Lee, Alexis Bighley, Cindy Browne, and Joyce and Emma Quarnstrom, for their unconditional love. The Andersen family, who have lovingly cared for Ben and forgave me the time I left Katherine at school.

The first trainers, Sue EckMaahs, Chris Burkett, Dean Bondhus, Sonja Gidlow, Shawna Egan, Tom Jacobs, and Michael Blanch.

Chris Bache, Tracy Howard, and Penba Tashi, for their wisdom and compassion in Tibet and my tent mate, Mary Tribble, for her infectious laugh and abundant joy.

And finally, my appreciation goes out to those at Career Press who helped this book find its way to print, including Mike Lewis, Michael Pye, Kristen Parkes, and Chris Carolei.

Contents

Introduction

The heart before you is a mirror.
See there your own form.

—Shinto saying

Modern civilization is teetering on the brink of an epidemic in "emotional-idiocy." Despite our collective concerns, negative emotions such as cynicism, irritability, anger, depression, and hostility are on the rise in our families, communities, and workplaces.

My clients realize they can no longer take workplace trust and respect for granted. Organizations are in desperate need of people who instinctively pull together during a crisis. We could all benefit from less toe-to-toe, and more side-by-side. Over the last 20 years I've helped hundreds of organizations develop strategies that protect cohesiveness and productivity from an increasingly irritable world.

Cohesive, trusting energy is dissipating in our society and world. Yet it is the *only source of energy* that sustains groups and allows the intellectual discipline that solves complex problems. This book is about understanding, and reversing, this disturbing trend.

In the following pages you will learn:
- ▷ Why hostility, exhaustion, and stress are on the rise in our society and workplaces.
- ▷ That 30 percent of bullying behavior is initiated by supervisors.
- ▷ How employees get even.

▷ The number of customers who take their business elsewhere after being treated with disrespect.

▷ Why smart leaders are taking steps to preserve internal trust and positive energy.

▷ How to develop an unflappable ability to manage, despite crises and chaos.

▷ The most important habit you bring to the table.

▷ How you can lower your stress level and enhance your health.

▷ The mind-boggling fiscal costs of "us vs. them" mentalities.

▷ Why focusing on systems, rather than people, saves organizations millions of dollars.

▷ Why belittling others is a common, low-skill, self-defeating way to bond.

▷ The root cause of hostility, and how to avoid "taking the bait."

▷ How to sidestep the self-defeating errors that are at the source of almost every workplace conflict, regardless of the setting, geographic location, or educational level of those involved.

▷ When you're most likely to be hooked by the dazzle of contempt.

▷ How your assumptions turn hurting, insecure people into adversaries, and leave *you* without a solution.

▷ Why hostility is self-fulfilling and often leads to depression.

▷ Why self-righteous indignation is fun, but toxic.

▷ Why yelling at others hurts *you.*

▷ How to break a Cycle of Contempt.

▷ The "glue" that will save your career from failed relationships, missed opportunities, and heartache.

▷ How nature rewards cooperation and altruism with feelings of pleasure.

▷ How to benefit from connectedness and its positive impact on health.

> ▷ The motivator that's driven us for thousands of years.

> ▷ The benefits of holding others accountable in a climate of *warmth*.

> ▷ How to earn and maintain the admiration and respect of direct reports, bosses, and peers.

> ▷ How to develop a reputation as a trustworthy, "can do" employee and leader.

It took me 20 years to identify and validate these insights and techniques. Fortunately, by reading this book, you can improve on my learning curve by quite a bit.

Contempt seduces even the brightest and best

Our lives are so saturated with frustration that *if we don't consciously determine how we are reacting, our reactions determine who we are*.

The daily blitz of aggravations and frustrations has become part and parcel of modern life in the form of unpopular decisions, disagreements, disappointments, and delays. How employees and leaders, in every sector of our society, respond to these aggravations and stressors is critical to our effectiveness and momentum.

In the following pages, you'll see that as frustration increases in intensity and frequency, so does irritability and "us vs. them" thinking.

Reflexive, blaming responses are arrogant, expensive, and privileged thieves that ignite power struggles and hostile factions. They accumulate status and clout, and transform what should be side-by-side problem-solving into ugly, toe-to-toe confrontations.

These accusatory reactions pilfer tangible and intangible assets: profit, opportunities, time, collaboration, passion, vitality, and trust. Individuals begin to exploit other people's errors and squander opportunities to build alliances.

> *Defensive and aggressive reactions to frustration*
> *Are the most costly, unmonitored vulnerabilities*
> *Of savvy and cost-conscious workforces.*

"Us vs. them" mentalities round up your valuables in broad daylight and walk out the front door. Blame is a gutsy con artist that weaves itself into the fabric of organizations with the naïve and oblivious support of employees and management. After you read this book, you will stop underwriting their operation.

Soft issues, hard price tag

During 20 years of consulting, the biggest fiscal payoffs I accrued for organizations occurred in groups that were failing due to conflict and its inevitable companion—stress. In fact, the following chapters contain two case studies where the principles outlined in this book saved organizations millions of hard-earned dollars.

Ending longstanding mistrust and negativity not only makes a walloping contribution to the budget, it also enhances customer satisfaction, employee well-being, retention, workflow, mood, momentum, the potency of leadership, and the success of new initiatives.

Imagine the payoffs when employees and leaders are able to *avoid* blame and turf wars.

Destructive disagreement shakes optimism and core beliefs

Accounts of workplace conflict are overheard in restaurants, airplanes, wedding receptions, and health clubs. They spill into our personal lives and permanently change our character.

Tales of lost loyalty, mistrust, and fear occur so frequently that most people believe these negative experiences are inevitable. We become fearful and observant about who's "in," who's "out," who's in the closed-door meeting, and who's going out for drinks after work.

We care passionately about our work, reputations, and status within our teams and groups. Stories about simmering conflict and workplace clashes are among the most dramatic experiences of modern life. We all have heard scores of stories of workplace conflict that carry the themes of depression, self-doubt, anger, and despair. Often the story is laced with self-righteousness and cynicism.

Superficially, these stories seem to be told because the teller wants someone to validate his or her point of view. However, at a deeper level, people are searching for answers to their core beliefs and assumptions about human nature.

We were friends for years, we trusted each other. What happened?

If the disagreement could destroy that relationship, are all my relationships at risk?

What do my direct reports and colleagues really *think about what I did?*

Do they understand my rationale?

Do they think I behaved callously?

Will I always feel this vulnerable?

Should I pull back from my work relationships and be more aloof?

Does the pain and self-doubt ever go away?

What could I have done differently?

Did I do the right thing?

Was I being unreasonable?

Were there options I couldn't see?

We deserve answers to these questions. We need to understand the dynamics of destructive conflict, invisible walls, and mistrust, not only to resolve them, but more importantly, to *avoid* them.

There are specific techniques you can use to avoid the fiscal and emotional costs of a mishandled conflict. With a few simple steps, you will be able to keep disagreement from taking center stage and fragmenting your team, department, organization, and family.

Bullying, blaming, and boors

Despite what we fear, bullying, hostility, and blame are *not* human nature. As you'll see in the stories that follow, personality is malleable. People's reactions are determined to a great extent by their settings, the norms of the group to which they belong, and the magnitude of perceived threat. When people feel threatened or lack skills, they react *reflexively*.

Reflexive reactions are often irrational. Frightened individuals strike out, push away, or jerk back. Individuals caught in the exchange of hostility express outrage about the behavior of those they are in conflict with, and privately question their own. Behaviors that conscientious people condemn in others suddenly seem justifiable for themselves.

We accuse others, and excuse ourselves.

—Unknown

Unfortunately, as fear escalates, people's reactions become more counterproductive and more destructive. The fallout of unresolved conflict triggers doubts about human nature and the viability of every relationship. These conclusions can be permanent. Stung by these experiences, people often decide that they should not trust again, nor invest in their direct reports, colleagues, and coworkers.

In the case studies that follow you'll see that hurt, not malice, is often at the root of conflict. The trigger for a destructive conflict often lies in an act, pattern of treatment, or callousness toward another person's loyalty, commitment, or investment.

When an individual feels that their concern for the well-being of their organization or team isn't valued, he or she often retreats behind an invisible wall that is easily misunderstood. Without information, bystanders and colleagues drift into a state of perpetual confusion and fear about the reasons underlying the demise of joint dreams.

No one wants to be excluded from the group

Negative, blaming reactions are explosive and contagious because *no one* wants to become a scapegoat and risk exclusion from the group. I am often struck by the passion with which people defend their reputations and behavior, and the pervasive drive to avoid exclusion.

The need to belong to a clan, family, gang, or workplace team is a powerful, ancient drive. Behavior that appears aggressive and unreasonable is often the attempt of an unskilled and desperate person who is struggling to stay within the workplace community, to be heard, and therefore *included.*

Leaders are not exempt from these struggles—in reality, they face additional, unique temptations. Leaders, who often draw their primary support from their direct reports rather than peers, often fall into the trap of using blame and ridicule of other departments and decision-makers as a means of building in-groups of loyal, unquestioning allies. Little do they realize that these mean-spirited behaviors are not only counterproductive, they are painfully transparent.

Within one or two experiences, employees learn how to bring data to the boss. They'll unconsciously choose between inflammatory, personality-based, and speculative means of delivery, or accurate, situation-based, and factual means. Employees learn quickly which one pleases the boss more.

The drive to resolve conflict is powerful and reliable

The energy that can build behind resolution and reconciliation is surprisingly powerful, and often easy to ignite. Even in highly adversarial settings, when I arrive to address the stress and fear in a workplace, employees and leaders grasp the alternative path with relief.

When work groups are presented with a route toward resolution, and a mere outline of a competent process, they pull together, suspend self-oriented needs, and arrive at our meetings with renewed optimism, and with their sleeves rolled up, ready to work and begin anew.

Individuals *want* to be connected in healthy, productive communities. Anthropologists tell us that cooperation is an ancient practice and is critical to adaptation. Healthy communities are our only means of achieving the goals that none of us can accomplish alone. The motivation exists. We need only provide the opportunity for its expression.

Ending workplace blame and mistrust is the first step of the journey. When you replace negative interactions with a climate of respect and appreciation, you and your organization hit the energy lottery.

Chapter One

The Self-Defeating Habits of Otherwise Brilliant People: Getting Duped by the Dazzle of Contempt

*Any intelligent fool can make things bigger, more complex
and more violent. It takes a touch of genius, and a lot of
courage, to move in the opposite direction.*

—Albert Einstein

We must begin to acknowledge that something central to civilization is threatening to unravel. Our economic, social, and environmental systems are becoming increasingly strained. Americans, Canadians, and Europeans are responding to unprecedented levels of stress and exhaustion. As individuals become overtaxed and anxious, two disparate views wrestle for their allegiance: hostility and compassion. In both our workplaces and our worlds, hostility and blame threaten rational decision-making and kindheartedness.

Reversing this trend in society is a daunting task. However, you can make your workplace a haven from, rather than an extension of, incivility and disrespect.

For our workplaces to thrive it's imperative that you understand the principles that underlie hostility and take steps to move your workplace in the opposite direction. Creating climates of hearty appreciation, where employees and management work in optimal health and productivity, takes commitment and skill.

Hostility is on the rise

Our society doesn't compile a comprehensive index of hostility levels. However, we can assess the rise of negativity and blame within our culture by scanning a list of assorted statistics.

▷ Twenty years ago there were a dozen vehement, shock-jock radio stations. In 2004 there were more than 1,000.

▷ The American Automobile Association reports that intentional driver-to-driver violence has increased 51 percent in the last decade.

▷ The National Highway Traffic Safety Administration now considers road rage the number one traffic problem. The U.S. Department of Transportation believes that two-thirds of fatalities are attributable to aggressive driving.

▷ SurfControl, which provides Website content filtering, found that Websites based on intolerance, hate, and graphic violence have increased 300 percent in the last 10 years.

▷ In a 2002 study by the Public Agenda Research Group, nearly eight out of 10 respondents said that lack of respect and courtesy is a serious national problem.

▷ The National Association of Sports Officials now offers assault insurance to members due the rising number of attacks on referees at professional and youth events.

▷ In 2002, Rasmussen Research found 80 percent of respondents feel that children display worse manners than in the past.

▷ The American Psychological Association found that 57 percent of the children under the age of 12 who are murdered are killed by one of their parents.

▷ Family members commit 30 percent of the murders of the elderly (60-plus years old).

▷ According to a study at the University of Wisconsin, Oshkosh, 66 percent of middle-school students, and 70 percent of elementary school students, say they have been bullied.

▷ Stress has become so epidemic that the UN declared it "the disease of the 20th century."

Although workplaces are insulated from changes in society, they are not, ultimately, immune. Workplaces mirror the emotions of a world that has become more frightening, and embodies a less certain future.

Why should Americans feel anxious and irritable? The aggregate wealth of Americans is at an all-time high. However, the Social Health Index of the United States, a composite measure of 16 indices (infant morality, child abuse, teenage suicide and drug use, high school drop-outs, poverty, homicides, affordable housing, and so on) has plummeted from a score of 73 in 1970, to 46 in 2001, a drop of 38 percent. In 2001 (the most current data), the score made its deepest decline since 1982, dropping eight out of a possible 100 points.

In schools, society, and workplaces, self-reported measures of exhaustion, economic insecurity, and rising stress result in a society that has become increasingly self-centered and uncivil. Whenever anxiety dominates a society, self-righteous indignation, irritability, and blame beckon with the false promise of justice and relief.

Irritability and hostility at work

A study in April 22, 1996 edition of *U.S. News & World Report* stated that 88 percent of Americans feel that lack of respect at work is a serious problem and is getting worse. According to an Integra Realty Resources survey, 42 percent of respondents stated that yelling, verbal abuse, and "desk rage" occurred at their place of work.

Workplace incivility is not limited to the United States. In studies done in both the United Kingdom and Canada, workers have expressed concern about rudeness and lack of respect at work. More than 50 percent of respondents in a UK study claimed they had been stressed at work to the point of wanting to fight back. In a study conducted in Toronto, 33 percent of nurses said in the previous five days of work they had been on the receiving end of verbal abuse by patients, doctors, or staff. In a 2003 study of 126 Canadian white-collar workers, 25 percent reported witnessing incivility daily, and half said they were targets of incivility at least once per week.

Incivility at work is subtler than workplace violence, and is often described as "emotional violence," "disrespect," "personality conflicts," "bullying," and "rudeness." As the costs and prevalence become more known, this issue receives increasing attention from researchers.

The majority of scholarly studies define workplace incivility as insidious, low-intensity hassles that violate norms for mutual respect. Surprisingly, these "micro-events" often have greater impact on stress than major, exceptional stressors.

Incivility includes behaviors such as: condescending and demeaning comments, overruling decisions without offering a reason, disrupting meetings, giving public reprimands, talking about others behind their back, giving others the silent treatment, ignoring people, rude comments, not giving credit, dirty looks, insulting others, and yelling.

Leaders aren't exempt from boorishness. In a study cited in the *Journal of Occupational Health Psychology*, one-third of aggressive workplace behaviors were initiated by the supervisor—becoming what one consultant called the emerging "workplace pariah."

According to Hafen, Frandsen, Kareen, and Hooker in *The Health Effects of Attitudes, Emotions and Relationships* (Benjamin Cummings, 2001), the most stressful interpersonal conflict at work occurs when an employee is in conflict with a supervisor and feels there is a lack of trust or that they are being treated unfairly or inconsiderately.

Customer Care Measurement and Consulting of Virginia found, in a national sampling, that 45 percent of respondents reported a serious consumer problem or complaint in the past year. Of that group, 70 percent said they experienced rage by the way the company handled the complaint. March Grainer, their chairman said, "Consumers today are more angry and hostile than they ever have been." More customers are using profanity and seeking a measure of revenge.

Stress, incivility, irritability, and rudeness

Rudeness and irritability appear to be connected to unrelenting stress and time urgency. Chronic strains are the most commonly cited causes of stress. In a Canadian study the most frequently cited stressors included: overwork, trying to do too much at once, not having enough money, worries about children, time pressures, a change in job for the worse, a demotion; a cut in pay, management changes, marital problems, and budget cuts.

Jed Diamond, author of *Irritable Men's Syndrome*, collected some remarkable data by posting a survey on the *Men's Health* Website to which 6,000 males, ages 10 to 75, responded. The results give an alarming snapshot of how many males "often" or "almost always" feel gloomy, negative, and hopeless (51 percent); feel sarcastic (54 percent); feel exhausted (43 percent); have a desire to get away from it all (62 percent); possess a strong fear of failure (55 percent); become impatient (57 percent); or experience sleep problems (51 percent).

In a recent Gallup poll, 80 percent of Americans reported feeling overworked and stressed due to company downsizing. In 1988, 22 percent of those polled worried about being laid off. According to an International Survey Research poll conducted 11 years later, that figure had doubled. In 1985, 16 percent of college freshman said they frequently felt overwhelmed by all they have to do. By 1999 the percentage jumped to 30 percent (Reuters, January 2000).

Got a minute?

When increased stress levels are combined with time pressures, good people reach the limits of composure and civil behavior.

The Princeton Theology Seminary conducted a classic study in the 1970s on the impact of "time urgency" on behavior. Of the theology students who were told they were late to give their sermon on the Good Samaritan, only 10 percent stopped to assist a shabbily dressed "victim" in need of assistance. In the "low hurry" group, 63 percent offered help. Situations shape how we behave.

Costs of incivility

When workplace incivility and rudeness are tolerated rather than addressed, it sends a signal throughout the organization that results in more serious problems.

In the 1999 article "Tit for Tat," published in the *Academy of Management Review*, researchers concluded that incivilities begin an "upward-spiraling process" of negative behaviors to increasingly serious levels. Workplace violence, the researchers concluded, is often the result of a culmination of "escalation patterns of negative interactions" between individuals.

In a University of North Carolina study, employees who were forced to work in negative climates reported that they got less done while fuming about it (50 percent); no longer did their best work (20 percent); became less committed (37 percent); thought about quitting (46 percent); or resigned (12 percent).

In a study by Cortina, Magley, Williams and Langhout appearing in *The Journal of Occupational Health Psychology* (January, 2001), workers who reported feeling harassed and verbally abused had lower satisfaction score with supervisors, coworkers, and "the job in general." They ceased their "good citizen" behaviors, had greater absenteeism and tardiness, and increased their retaliation and aggressive behaviors. They showed greater anxiety, depression, and productivity declines, and increased disability claims. Both women and men became more distressed as incivility became more frequent; however, men became more distressed than women.

In an article published in a 2005 issue of *The Academy of Management Executive*, by Christine Pearson and Christine Porath, one in eight people who see themselves as targets of incivility at work leave their places of employment and most do not report the reason for their departure. A few will steal; some will sabotage equipment; and most will tell their friends, family, and colleagues how poorly they've been treated.

Clearly, there is no rest for the rude. Even employees with less power retaliate—but in ways that are undetectable. Pearson and Porath found that low status employees retaliate by spoiling the offending individual's reputation, spreading rumors, withholding information, covertly botching tasks, and delaying actions. Of those studied, 50 percent tell a more powerful colleague about the incivility they have suffered. Many tell peers and direct reports, who then search for their own ways to get even.

As levels of incivility rise, so do stress levels. The medical ailments that are linked with stress include arthritis, back problems, chronic bronchitis, stomach ulcers, heart disease, asthma, and migraines. No wonder absenteeism, tardiness, sick leave, and medical disability claims are increasing!

Time urgency, worries about children and finances, marital problems, exhaustion, and feeling overextended and anxious at work, translate into organizations in need of strategies for coping with anger, incivility, and the skills associated with maintaining composure.

Workplaces reflect the emotions of a world that has become more frightening and less secure, and they can play a significant role in the cure. They are more flexible and self-determined than government. They don't need legislation to act. They are also one of the few places where large numbers of adults have access to new ideas and the opportunity to develop skills.

Predictable, pervasive errors

If you ask a group to identify their worst workplace traumas, incivility and unresolved conflict would likely be near, or at, the top of their lists. When hostility and mistrust contaminate interactions between people or departments, no aspect of work is unaffected: collaboration stops, problem-solving becomes ineffective and biased, information is distorted, conversations become malicious, and speculation is negative. When a workforce becomes obsessed with building invisible walls, opportunities for improvement and growth are abandoned. Self-oriented behavior becomes the norm.

Destructive conflict ends long-standing friendships, brilliant partnerships wither, and good people leave, hedging about their reasons. Paranoia replaces passion, cynicism replaces commitment, fears dull enthusiasm and pride. People lay low and dig in. When being visible is too big of a risk, creativity and entrepreneurship suffer. Judgment declines and the capacity for decision-making becomes impaired.

None of these costs of conflict are calculated off the bottom line. I have found this phenomenon to be true regardless of the setting, including universities, factories, banks, fire stations, marketing firms, mental health clinics, Fortune 500 companies, faith communities, machine shops, law firms, police departments, forensic prisons, and the IRS.

My first efforts at addressing workplace irritability and conflict were burdened by widely accepted beliefs about the nature of mistrust, camaraderie, and commitment. Early on I assumed that resolving conflict consisted of sorting out good guys from bad guys, and I imagined myself correcting and reprimanding the self-centered, pig-headed, and arrogant. I expected to find "innocents" in need of protection from the malicious. I assumed root causes were idiosyncratic and unique.

None of these expectations were useful. I learned that I had to let go of my assumptions and allow myself to be surprised by the actual underpinnings of mistrust and tension.

In reality, most conflicts are the results of predictable errors made by very conscientious, well-intentioned people. Surprisingly, and somewhat annoyingly, I found the same patterns in my own behavior. At first I was flabbergasted. Then I became amused by my human failings. Eventually, I felt grateful and relieved because I could look back over my life and see where making these mistakes had cost me moments of sanity, harmed relationships, and hurt my effectiveness in work. Now I consider these insights the most treasured of friends because they bring me unending opportunities to avoid negativity and anger by choosing how I think. They allow me unprecedented effectiveness, even with my crabbiest clients.

However, I discovered that most people were at the bottom of the same learning curve. Consequently, when conflict escalates, almost all organizations underreact. I've found the lag time between the onset of destructive conflict and a call for help ranges between 18 months and two years. Many leaders don't know what to do, and hope that if they look the other way the conflict will burn itself out. Sometimes it appears their strategy has worked and the tension disappears. However, if you probe below the superficial calm, many times peace has been restored only because at least one valuable person has left—or has stayed on the job and withdrawn their passion and investment.

When conflict doesn't burn out and stays hot and disruptive, leaders often ask for help reluctantly. In best-case scenarios, a competent consultant arrives and provides the skills the organization lacks. Often we complete assessments, teach, consult, tease, encourage, reassure, and challenge. Groups reach resolution, and normalcy is restored. However, roughly two years of difficult, painful times have passed, and people, profit, and productivity have suffered deeply.

Don't just resolve destructive conflict—eliminate it!

I began to wonder if it was possible to help people avoid triggers to irritability and mistrust. Would people be interested in learning how to avoid workplace tension and blame? Was there a way to transfer my insights during periods of relative calm? I offered my first seminars.

The results were astonishing. I've been teaching seminars for 15 years to thousands of people across the United States and Europe. Participants repeatedly tell me how much they've learned, both immediately after keynotes and seminars, and, more importantly, years later.

Recently, a client described me as "An angel of enlightenment" two years after she heard me speak. Pretty strong, I thought, but then I realized we had worked together in Alaska, where people don't get much sun.

I wish I could tell you that I came up with these ideas on a slow-moving train to the West Coast. In reality, everything in this book came from two memorable and rewarding decades of working alongside clients who trusted me with painful workplace disappointments, as well as feelings of betrayal, confusion, and fear. They trusted me with their fragile hope and together we succeeded, despite the mythology about difficult people, jerks, and malice.

Duped by the dazzle of contempt

The behaviors that actually do get us in trouble aren't hard to observe because they are *everywhere*. When conflict escalates, most people are so busy scrutinizing other people's behavior that they overlook their own. In fact, the real triggers to destructive conflict are so common that most of us consider the behaviors normal, maybe even clever.

The trigger of the downward spiral usually begins when individuals belittle someone else, in order to sidestep or minimize their own disappointing outcomes, to look superior, or to bond with others in their group. Sometimes slights are delivered with a mere roll of the eyes, a shrug, or an audible sigh. Blame and denigration are surprisingly tolerated, encouraged, excused, planned around, and explained away. In some workplaces the ability to make witty "cuts" toward a colleague or supervisor seems to be admired.

Most people believe that mean-spirited reactions are witty and justified. They believe biting retorts or feigned resignation to another person's "stupidity" is useful and clever.

However, two years later, when everyone else has left the party, I'm down in the trenches with these otherwise clever people, helping them pick up the pieces of their relationships and tarnished careers. Well-manicured people with MBAs, astronomical IQs, and Ph.D.s make this mistake. How does this happen?

We are duped by the dazzle of contempt. Indignation and aggressive reactions seem like reasonable responses if you observe the situation for the short-term. And unfortunately, the negative repercussions of denigrating others—which you'll read about in detail in Chapter Five—are hidden and delayed.

There's another problem with cutting sarcasm and ridicule. The "payoffs" are so much fun. A good zinger draws a crowd and a guffaw. It's aggressive, it's adrenaline, and it's a kick.

However, once you become aware of the invisible costs of contempt you'll be *very* motivated to unplug from it. And there's another incentive to forgo contempt for effectiveness: cooperation feels good. Respectful, validating behavior toward others is rewarding. It feeds our higher aspirations and inspires others to meet our expectations. Additionally, it allows us to feel proud of our behavior and feel more like honorable human beings.

Blame and turf wars are not human nature

If we fail to stem the tide of negativity, our collective future is frightening. Imagine a society that becomes more and more dominated by incivility, disrespect, negative assumptionism, and cynicism.

A lot of people are resigned to the increased hostility in our workplaces, families, schools, and society at large. Some fear it's inevitable. Many people think that civility and respectful behavior toward others is passé, old-fashioned, or a remnant of a more innocent time that we'll not see again. But no one wants hostility.

As you'll see, blame, turf wars, and destructive conflict are not human nature. We don't have to roll over and allow negativity to roll over us. We now understand how to turn the tide away from blame and aggression.

> *Discovering the new frontiers of peace is an inside job....It's time to rely on individual responsibility, which comes from being more responsible for your own energies.*

—Doc Childe, *Transforming Stress*

I've used the ideas you'll read about in this book in more than 120 very tricky and very troubled situations where trust had been broken and individuals had lost hope. Many of my clients were surprised by how quickly we were able to restore collaboration. Conflict and blame can be transformed into respect and cooperation. These principles work.

Trench-validity and stickiness

You may believe that it's possible for people to learn new ways of behaving—but do people maintain their gains?

A managing director in the United Kingdom (the equivalent of a CEO in the United States) told me that even though he's received three promotions and changed offices multiple times, he still uses my materials and keeps them in the top drawer of his desk. When he told me this, it had been seven years since he heard me speak.

Dozens of times, when I've returned to a client site for a new project or to conduct another seminar, attendees from past years proudly lead me back to their work areas where handouts from the seminar are still hanging. It's common for me to get e-mails from people years after I've been on-site to tell me how they still use the techniques. These ideas stick.

People are willing to try the techniques because they offer a less violent way of handling disagreements, disappointment, and delays. Competent responses to frustration improve self-confidence and enhance health. They resonate with our desires to be appreciated and to appreciate. They appeal to our better nature and demonstrate how we can make permanent gains in profitability and productivity. These habits build tenacious friendships and sweeten the workplace with warmth.

The only thing people have to let go of is that nasty, vindictive jolt of energy that comes from blame and self-righteous indignation. It's a small loss compared to the ocean of positive energy that we can then embrace.

Frustration and "heart hassles"

Let's return to the idea that stress and time urgency are straining our ability to treat each other with respect. In my work I've found that frustration is the most common trigger of negative emotions, stress, and hostility at work.

Frustrations can be caused by the high drama that accompanies major project deadlines or the minutia of day-to-day activities. Aggravations come in the form of ongoing interruptions, missed sales targets, lost files, patient noncompliance, wrong parts, computer crashes, missed planes, stalled projects, faulty data, last-minute changes, misunderstandings, resource shortages, and so on.

Frustration is constant, and unless we get on top of it, the residue of each individual annoyance accrues and mounts. For instance, imagine you miss a critical deadline with a customer because your colleague, Sam, fails to provide a critical piece of data. You wince when you see that the terse e-mail you receive from your customer is copied to your boss. Your neck muscles tense, then you play a few rounds of e-mail damage control with Sam.

You stay late trying to make it right with your customer, appease your boss, and do damage control with your colleague. You leave work later than you planned and do a slow burn on the way home during the height of rush-hour traffic. You receive a cool reception and a cold meal from your disgruntled family. Your mood is lousy, you snap at the kids. You feel unappreciated and your evening is tanked. You wake up at 4 a.m. with stress-induced insomnia and arrive at work exhausted, carrying over the negativity of the previous day's work.

Incidences of frustration are not discrete and separate. A poorly handled frustration in the morning sets you up physiologically for increasingly negative reactions when the next frustration hits. When people don't handle aggravations well, they not only make the next one more difficult to manage, they damage relationships as they go, and their personal and professional networks begin to unravel. They no longer have access to warmth, laughter, goofiness, light-hearted chatter, compassionate advice, and friendly sounding boards. Life becomes harsh and barren.

Having a skill set that allows employees and leaders to maintain mood and momentum during periods of high stress and frustration is a critical life proficiency. Yet, for some reason, our ability to manage frustration is seldom addressed. I've asked hundreds of attendees if they've ever been in a seminar or read a book on handling frustration, and less than 1 percent of the audience responds in the affirmative. Yet, frustration is one of the most predictably disruptive aspects of modern life.

Charles Stroebel, M.D., in *QR: The Quieting Reflex*, reports that we suffer approximately 30 "heart hassles" a day. He describes these as moments of "irritating, frustrating, or distressing mini-crises." If you multiple that by 365 days in a year, during the course of 70 years, it comes to more than 750,000 in a lifetime! Despite this frequency most people have paid little, if any, attention to how they respond to delays, disagreements, and disappointments, and the impact of their reactions on their relationships, health, and success. You can multiply that number by every employee, leader, client, customer, supplier, and family member. No wonder so many people report they're at a breaking point at work!

It's critical to be aware of how you react to frustration, because every one of your responses creates positive or negative repercussions that accumulate throughout your day and lifetime. However, if you're like most (otherwise brilliant) people, you've never thought about the importance of your reactions when you hit a hurdle or delay.

Three cultures at work: Hostile, helpless, and hearty appreciation

Every time we face frustration, the way we think about it, not the event itself, determines how frustrated we feel and how effectively we respond. Most people are unaware that they continuously and unconsciously answer the question, "Why am I frustrated?"

You probably gravitate toward one or two of three basic reactions to this question, which begin to operate like reinforced circuitry in your mind.

The first response to frustration is reflexive and inflammatory, and it targets other people as the source of problems. This automatic response undermines efforts, cinches long-term failure, and increases hostility.

Think of a time when you've been in a highly charged, blaming culture at your place of work, family, faith community, country club, special interest group, or sports team. What words would you use to describe the atmosphere? Participants in seminars use words such as tense, frightening, hateful, irrational, destructive, foolish, wasteful, tragic, and stupid. Imagine the impact on performance!

Although these environments are loaded with adrenaline and cortisol, and appear to provide powerful advantages, in the next chapter you'll discover the hefty, toxic price we pay every time we tap the energy of aggression in response to an aggravation.

The second reaction is a form of harsh self-criticism, and it typically begins to dominate thinking after the adrenaline response fades. This reaction turns the power of contempt inward. It causes individuals to withdraw, become depressed, and feel helpless or immobile. As you'll see, it increases the risk factor for a variety of illnesses. Self-loathing results in the loss of energy and triggers feelings of lethargy and hopelessness. Participants describe these emotions as boring, stifling, oppressive, mind-numbing, and draining. Some work situations are so void of stimulation and energy that employees struggle with inertia, isolation, and depression.

Think of a time when you worked or lived in a culture dominated by apathy or boredom. How did it feel? How did it affect your productivity?

The third response to frustration is a reflective reaction, and when problems occur, this thinking pattern focuses on situations, not the people. It's an analytical but warm reaction to frustration that makes climates hearty, and increases respect, influence, resiliency, productivity, and a sense of well-being. Reactions that support people as they tackle hard problems increase positive energy and sustain groups through thick and thin. In describing these climates, participants in seminars use words such as productive, fun, energizing, creative, wacky, surprising, respectful, and affirming. As you'll see, these atmospheres are loaded with advantages.

Figure 1. Three cultures at work

In Chapter Three you'll learn that not only does a positive orientation increase your effectiveness, it can prolong your life and decrease your risk for developing deadly diseases. In addition, you'll look at data that suggests we are "hardwired" to be connected to others. For instance, cooperation stimulates the part of the brain that is associated with feelings of pleasure. Most of us do our best work when we're tapped into the positive energy of camaraderie and accomplishment. This is what a software designer recently described as "being in the zone" with his work and colleagues.

If health, success, mood, loyal colleagues, and dedicated direct reports are high on your list of priorities, your choice will be easy. However, it takes commitment, courage, and skill to create and sustain positive energy in groups.

Our first responses to frustration were probably determined within our family of origin. When I poll people in seminars, roughly 10 percent say they were raised in families that had high standards and expectations but were consistently positive, warm, and supportive. The other remaining 90 percent place their families in the indifferent or hostile categories. I'm not surprised. Where and when do we have an opportunity to learn the skills that are necessary to create hearty groups that withstand increasing amounts of pressure, frustration, and exhaustion?

I think about these three emotions—hostility, helplessness, and hearty appreciation—on a continuum as shown in Figure 1 on page 32. At the left end are the negative emotions such as irritability, cynicism, and hostility. In the middle are depression and isolation—withdrawal from work and colleagues, a sense of helplessness and resignation. At the right end are vigor, camaraderie, respect, and the spirit of problem-solving.

There's a vertical scale, that measures the amount of energy these emotions create. On this scale, energy is low at the bottom and high at the top. You can see two peaks of energy, at the negative and positive poles, and the loss of energy in middle.

HeartMath, a nonprofit research organization in Boulder Creek, California, uses biofeedback data to help their clients understand and manage their anger. Although our two organizations do very different work, we came to the same conclusion—there are two primary sources of energy: frustration and appreciation. On page 34 is an electrocardiogram (ECG) of electrical frequencies that were observed while monitoring biofeedback data. In the energy caused by frustration there are

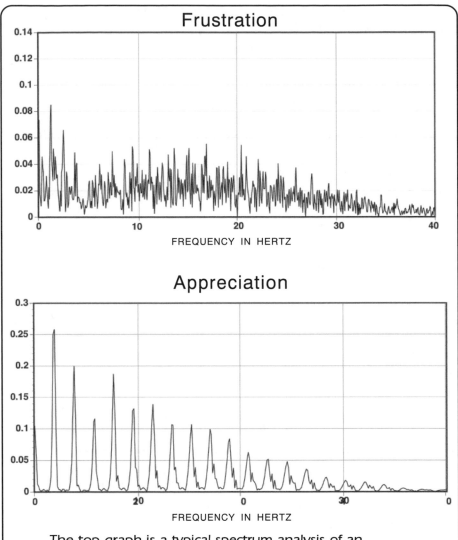

The top graph is a typical spectrum analysis of an electrocardiogram (ECG) of a person experiencing frustration. This is called an incoherent spectrum because the frequencies are scattered and disordered.

The bottom graph shows the frequency analysis of the ECG of a person experiencing deep, sincere appreciation. This is called a coherent spectrum because the power is ordered and harmonious.

Figure 2. Frustration and Appreciation ECGs

extreme variations in heart rhythms. The body is working hard, but it is not in synch. HeartMath calls this the rhythm incoherent. I think about it as a hardworking engine badly in need of a tune-up.

The heart variations in deep, sincere appreciation indicate coherence in the body and an alignment of energy linked to optimal performance. In this state, the cardiovascular, immune, hormonal, and nervous systems function efficiently. We experience greater mental clarity and creativity. We'll refer to these two differences throughout the book.

When I work with high-conflict teams I think about these two variations because my goal is to help teams progress from the left to the right poles, as tension decreases and problems are resolved.

The energy at the left end is dramatic, loud, and manic. It's a rush, but almost everyone hates the feelings of anger and hostility.

However, the middle emotion, indifference, is worse. Both the left and center emotions feel lousy, but at least at the left end people have enough energy to get out of bed. With indifference (which can morph into depression) people feel lousy and they lack energy. Consequently, I've learned that when I'm working with teams, I can't simply reduce tension, resolve the problems, and walk away. I have to stay with the group until it is hooked by the energy of camaraderie and achievement. Once they get hooked on the buzz of collaboration and commitment my work is almost done. Once they're reconnected, they solve the problems with relative ease. You might think it unlikely they would be able to sustain positive energy, but the other two options are so miserable that they are actually very careful about preserving their positive gains.

When I'm consulting with high-conflict groups, we document our agreements and create a fall-back plan if any party fails to uphold their commitments. In the 120 conflicts I've facilitated, only once have I had to return to a client site and reopen a conflict that I thought we had resolved.

People think I'm a wizard when former enemies turn into allies. In reality, I've tapped the innate, human desire to be connected. As you'll see, people are aching for the energy of camaraderie and achievement. I just remove the barriers.

In which category would you put your team?

As you've been reading, you might be wondering which of the three categories you (or your team) might fall: negative, indifferent, or positive.

Groups and individuals move to the left (hostility) and right (positive energy) depending on how stressed, exhausted, relaxed, or threatened they feel. However, most teams have a set point that's a fairly good average of tone. If it's not immediately obvious where you fall on this continuum as an individual, imagine where you would put your closest friends. It's likely your orientation is similar.

If you or your team gets energy from hostility and contempt, blames people for problems, trusts only a few people (or select groups), views others as adversaries, believes that life is a race to get others before they get you, then your hostile, paranoid feelings and interactions with others will confirm your beliefs.

Similarly, if you and your colleagues believe that we are essentially alone, that life is stupid, that effort often goes unrewarded, and that withdrawal from other people and opportunities is inevitable, then your isolation and lack of recognition will confirm your beliefs.

On the other hand, if you or your group works hard to build and earn mutual respect, does what it takes to achieve established goals, gets a thrill from learning and solving problems, and reaches out to others in times of need, then the social capital created will confirm your collective beliefs.

Each of these three choices (hostility, depression, and appreciation), are validated by the people around you and by your combined life experiences. We unconsciously seek out people with similar orientations.

In most workplace lunchrooms you can watch people unwittingly sort themselves into groups with similar outlooks. There's the cynical, hostile group, bonded with contempt for others (and others in their group when they're not present). There's usually a group looking fairly deflated and depressed—disconnected from what's swirling about them. And then there's a group that is warm and friendly. They're reaching out, building networks, and gathering and giving information.

Although each group has a very different view of their workplace and world, each group validates the orientation and assumptions of its members. They're all looking at the same external world. The difference in their perceptions can be traced back to differences in their thinking.

A director of a state agency who has worked under many different commissioners unknowingly summed up the difference between the first and third approach by telling me: "Some of our commissioners come out to field during a crisis, and their goal is to punish people. They immediately create climates of fear and tension. When these commissioners arrive, people scatter.

"Other commissioners seek to understand how the problem occurred. They express appreciation for people's efforts and invite others to join in problem-solving. When they arrive, everyone pitches in to get at the root cause of the snafu. My direct reports love working for the latter, and hate working for the former."

Outside of work, our worldviews are reinforced by the kind of job, entertainment, music, friends, and colleagues that we gravitate toward. There are so many opportunities to tap into these different perspectives that we unconsciously begin to narrow where we focus our attention.

If you scan radio and TV programs, you'll find lots of broadcasts that cater to the reflexive, inflammatory energy of contempt. These programs inflame self-righteousness, hostility, and blame, which may draw a crowd but can't solve anything. They're only good for tearing down people and their efforts.

We can also find stations that provide listeners with a more reflective approach. In these broadcasts the producers seek to uncover the reasons underlying world and domestic events. These programs are driven by the possibility of resolving problems. They are dedicated to creating connections and solutions.

These differences reflect very different thinking patterns that we'll look at closely in the following pages. When we don't pay attention to how we think, our automatic responses often determine how we feel and behave. Our thinking patterns even determine what we experience. The following parable speaks well to this point.

What you find in the village ahead

A traveler, walking along a dusty road, sees an elderly man sitting by the roadside. Abruptly he shouts, "Hey! Old man! What are the people like in the next village?"

The old man responds by asking, "What did you find in the village you just left?"

"Scoundrels," the traveler grumbles, "we drank and gambled, and in the middle of the night someone stole my food!"

"Ah," says the old man wisely, "that's what you'll find in the village ahead."

A short time later, another traveler, on the same route between the same villages, approaches the elderly man.

"Tell me," the traveler asks kindly, "what kind of people will I find in the village ahead?"

The old man responds again, "What did you find in the village you just left?"

"Oh," responds the traveler, with obvious merriment, "I really enjoyed them! They were intelligent and generous. We told stories about our journeys and shared our simple meals."

"Ah," the old man replied, "That's what you'll find in the village ahead."

The sage understood that we create our realities through subtle, ongoing choices that reinforce our worldviews. These choices lead us to the experiences that we unconsciously anticipated, and will find again.

The most important habit you bring to the table

After years of working with both successful and troubled teams, I realized that the vast majority of people are oblivious to the three responses I just described, and the important role those reactions play in shaping our lives. Most of us want to have positive experiences but, for reasons we'll discuss in the next chapter, our reactions tend to be more hostile than warm when we are frustrated. This is especially true if we are reacting to frustrations without realizing that we have a choice.

Your automatic responses to frustration are the most important habit you bring to the table, in your workplace, family, and community. If you are a leader, in any aspect of your life, this is especially true.

Contempt is growing in our society and workplaces. However, because people in seminars jump at the opportunity to reduce their personal levels of hostility, I believe most individuals want this to change. All we need are the tools.

Chapter Two

Anger Makes You Stupid, Lonely, *and* Depressed: The Stinky Twins— Blaming Others, Blaming Self

A healthy brain exists to carry out your instructions—
you are the composer, it is your instrument.
—Deepak Chopra, M.D., *Peace is the Way*

During a seminar, I was discussing the physiology of positive and negative energy, and Bruce, a participant, had been riveted to his seat. Now that we were on break, he couldn't stop talking.

Bruce told me he was a Vietnam veteran still struggling from the trauma of combat and reflexive, aggressive reactions to frustration and threat. "In one morning of listening to you I've learned more about managing anger, and the reasons behind my irrational behavior, than I've learned in 20 years of outpatient therapy at the VA," he said.

Three years later we saw each other again. Bruce walked into a seminar I was teaching and sat in the back. On break he came over, excited to tell me his good news. "Anna, when I met you I was exhausted from a life that was filled with tension and conflict. I was beginning to feel that death was the only way to peace. But sitting in your seminar I realized there is a totally different way to look at the world, and since then I've made tremendous progress."

He shifted in his chair and leaned forward, before continuing, "In fact, I was elected leader of my service organization! That's how far I've come!

"Recently, during a meeting, one of the members got agitated and started yelling. I was able to calm him down using the methods you taught us. And then, to my surprise, I realized the entire room was calm—everyone was more relaxed and yet, people were animated. The energy was at the ceiling when we adjourned!

"And then the greatest thing of all happened. I realized I was the one who did it. I realized I could create the positive energy I needed so desperately. I didn't need to depend on anyone else to do it for me.

"I'm not afraid anymore! Coming to your class was the beginning of this shift, and I will never forget you."

When we met, Bruce was on a mission—to regain his inherent right to positive connections and feelings about himself and others. He not only developed new skills in controlling his anger, he learned he could also manage anger in others. With these new competencies he was able to generate positive energy with the people and projects he valued.

The previous chapter contained a brief overview of the three responses to frustration. In this chapter we'll focus on the two reflexive responses that had been Bruce's nemesis: blaming others and blaming self. As you'll see, blaming others when you are frustrated not only makes you hostile, but as Bruce intimately knew, it makes you more vulnerable to exhaustion and depression.

I'm frustrated and it's your fault!

Blaming others when facing one of your 750,000 frustrations (as discussed in Chapter One), is giving your brain the command to "search for stupidity in someone else!" You assume someone else caused your frustration: a peer, a boss, another department, or a colleague who snubbed you in yesterday's meeting.

The chilling reality of this approach is that your brain *will* find data that makes the other person look irrational and unreasonable. In a manner similar to searching for data on Google, once you limit your "search" to negative perceptions, your mind will present only data that fits your search criteria. (Figure 3.)

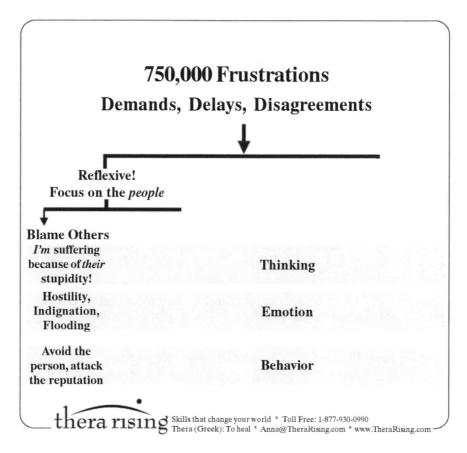

Figure 3. Frustration: arrow to "blame others"

For a dramatic example of how compliant our brains become once we see someone in a negative light, read "Transforming the Enemy" in the appendix. It's a very revealing story of how I struggled for seven years with a seemingly insurmountable problem, only to discover that part of the problem lay between my ears.

When searching for blame, our thoughts will focus on "who," not "why," and they will sound similar to, "I wouldn't be bringing work home tonight if my boss wasn't such a suck-up." "The board rejected our proposal because the members are totally out of touch with the market!" "The human resources coordinator is a bleeding heart!" "How can I get a decent day's work out of the low-lifes she keeps referring to me?"

Hitler and reflexive, irrational response to frustration

The importance of this subtle pattern can't be overstated. Hitler's reign over Nazi Germany is a classic example of a leader who stayed rigidly transfixed to the machinery of blame. He pitched his ideology to a frustrated, humiliated populace. Germans were not only frustrated by years of economic depression, they were bitter about the restitutions imposed following WWI. Germany lost land, colonies, the right to maintain an army, and were saddled with crushing penalties. Germans felt trapped and hopeless.

Hitler preached his beliefs to a disillusioned and emasculated audience. Early on he blamed Germany's problems on the developmentally and physically disabled, Catholics, gypsies, homosexuals, and Jews. He claimed they were a drain on society.

Hitler stayed true to his distorted thinking despite its explosive consequences and lack of impact on solving the economic crises. His legacy paints a clear portrait of the futility and irrationality of blaming people—especially for complex systemic problems.

Fortunately, Franklin D. Roosevelt was the political leader of the United States during the critical years of the Depression. In Chapter Three we'll look at his approach, which is a classic example of the more reflective, and effective, thinking pattern.

Inflammatory thinking and flooding

Blaming others for problems ignites frustrations. Individuals who use inflammatory thinking exaggerate the significance and pervasiveness of the inconvenience (Figure 4).

Examples of inflammatory thinking include:

I can't stand this! Why is the coffee pot always empty?!

Just my luck to have my computer crash now! Those idiots in information technology (IT)!

She's purposely avoiding me—just to make me look bad!

Figure 4: Inflammatory thinking

In this chapter I'll introduce three situations where blame and inflammatory thinking took center stage. In Chapter Three we'll return to these stories to see how the behavior of the key players changed when they analyzed their situation using a different thinking pattern.

The first case study involves an entire company simultaneously engaged in inflammatory, blame-based thinking in response to an unanticipated and surprising announcement.

Tony was an attorney in a corporate legal department of a manufacturing firm. The president had called a company-wide staff meeting to update the 200-plus employees on his plan to acquire a new facility. Once the staff had gathered, the audience was stunned when the owner announced that instead of acquiring a new building, he had decided to close the Minneapolis office and move the entire operation to his hometown in South Carolina.

The owner's reasons for the sudden shift were vague. The president tried to reassure the audience by saying the "brightest and best" would be invited to relocate, but the rest of the workforce would soon be without jobs. Tony's colleagues walked back to their departments in shock. Within a few minutes, their surprise turned into outrage, anger, and blame.

Tony, who had developed solid relationships with almost every division in the company, spent the next hour walking through the facility and listening as his colleagues spewed out their hostility. The engineers turned against their traditional foe, marketing: "This is marketing's fault! They dropped the ball on acquiring new markets."

As he wandered into the next division, Tony heard equally angry reactions in the sales group, aimed at engineering: "I told the engineering department to back down! But they didn't listen. They kept adding features to our products that drove our costs sky-high. Korea and Japan didn't help either! They've bulldozed their way into the American market!"

As Tony wandered back to the legal department he saw his colleagues huddled in a circle, centered on their own speculations about whom to blame: "The owner is selfish and probably returning to his home state to hunt and fish! He's your typical callous executive, thinking only of himself."

This situation is a perfect example of blame-based thinking, where each individual seeks to place blame for frustration on another party. Emotional reactions aren't the only aspect of the problem. As Tony's colleague's thinking inflamed, *so did their bodies.* This reaction to anger is called flooding because when stressed, our bodies *flood* with cortisol and adrenaline, and the heart beat increases. Under the influence of inflammatory thinking, behavior becomes irrational.

In the blame orientation, the problem is someone else's fault; therefore, the solution is beyond reach. Because inflammatory, blame-based thinking eliminates your ability to see options, you feel trapped. Your body reacts with aggression and activates the fight-or-flight response. Blame leads to emotional and physical arousal because inflammatory thinking has activated stress hormones, turning a minor inconvenience into a perception that this injustice is intolerable!

Unless you are facing physical danger, and speed and strength are important assets, flooding is counterproductive.

When individuals in the workplace use blame and inflammatory thinking, they often express their aggression in cold, subtle ways. Withdrawal, hoarding information, ostracizing, or "forgetting" to inform someone of an important meeting are passive forms of aggression. Aggression seldom results in *physical* attacks at work. When individuals are determined to damage a colleague, direct report, or supervisor, they do so verbally and attack their competence and character—two traits that people guard diligently.

Contempt contaminates employees and clients

When conflict between leaders escalates, it not only damages their relationship, it traumatizes the organization and customers. For example, imagine Rhonda, the vice president (VP) of sales, is frustrated with the slow response from operations, and makes a cutting remark about the VP of operations, Ted. She might directly criticize his motives or competence to her staff, and privately complain to a board member or CEO.

It is inevitable that her negative accusations will leak back to Ted, and Rhonda's comments will trigger a vicious cycle of negativity. Within the organization, colleagues will spread what she has said and it will eventually leak to close customers.

In an attempt to appease frustrated customers, sales employees will insinuate that operations is dropping the ball. When a customer raises this issue with Ted, he will be furious. He will know that his reputation is at stake and he must act to regain his standing. However, he will not go directly to Rhonda. He will attempt to discredit her by spreading negative accusations about her work and character.

Employees will pick up and amplify negative attitudes and rumors, and, as a result, they bring distorted or filtered data back to their supervisors.

When Ted and Rhonda discover that their mistrust and dislike for each other permeates their departments, their negative assumptions will appear justified. Ted will think, "It's not just me who's having problems with Rhonda. Both of my direct reports complain about the same issues." Rhonda will be receiving similar confirmations about her dislike for Ted.

Employees mirror a supervisor's mistrust as an act of loyalty, not malice. They want their boss and department to be aware of any possible threat.

If *anyone* within the team dares to break ranks and make a positive statement about the other group, *their* team will immediately reframe the *targeted party's* behavior as an act of manipulation.

Ted and Rhonda will continue to elevate their power struggle and subtly lobby their peers and CEO to adopt a negative perspective of the other person or group. Now every tidbit of negative information becomes a commodity. Ted and Rhonda will distort what is known and assume or fabricate what isn't. Each of them will attempt to bias more members to join their side and take a position against the other party.

If you were to sit in on one of their meetings a few months later, the executive team will look as if they had circled their wagons and were shooting inward!

Again, most power struggles aren't triggered by the intention to do harm. These conflicts are the result of passionate, well intended, and caring individuals who are unaware of the destructive nature of seemingly benign, and certainly common, behaviors.

When individuals are chronically overtaxed and feel besieged by workplace demands, blaming behaviors become automatic responses. Rhonda and Ted can't see three months down the road to where their snide comments will take them. However, if they act reflexively, their views of the world will narrow and they will eventually see each other as enemies needing to be conquered at any cost.

After being treated with disrespect, 60 percent of customers take their business elsewhere

The manner in which employees treat customers is determined, in part, by the norms for handling internal conflict and frustration. If the boss uses anger, sarcasm, and put-downs when he or she is frustrated with direct reports, it sends a clear message to customers about what he or she will consider justifiable.

However, customers have more options than employees, and they don't tolerate being treated with disrespect. A survey by Eticom in Columbia, South Carolina, found that 60 percent of customers take their business elsewhere when they are treated rudely by an employee—even if they have to drive further or pay more for the same service! Even more disturbingly, 75 percent of disgruntled customers walk away without telling a manager or supervisor why the company has lost their business. Customer Care Measurement and Consulting of Virginia found that more than 10 percent of disgruntled customers get even by complaining on an online bulletin board or chat room.

Predictable workplace targets and scapegoats

When the thinking patterns of blame and contempt take over an organization, no one is safe. Individuals or entire groups are targeted for any conceivable reason. Traditional targets include sales, operations, budgeting, information services, purchasing, the night shift, new hires, the union, customers, the parent company, the plant in Kentucky,and so on. Frontline workers blame a boss or the CEO, and the CEO blames the board. Architects blame project managers, city councils blame the mayor, support staff blames administration, firefighters blame headquarters, branch offices blame corporate, corporate blames field staff, and so on.

Anger is a feeling; hostility is an attitude

I've watched many leaders foolishly attempt to create team cohesiveness through hostility and denigration of other people or departments with statements such as, "Those jerks in sales don't care if we make a profit off this order!" Hostility is used as the "sugar high" of groups. It is quick and easy, and it is widely utilized in highly frustrated climates, because channeling anger toward a convenient target takes little effort or skill. However, this reflexive response only *appears* to meet the needs of employees and coworkers.

The more frequently we encourage or tolerate anger in response to frustration, the more likely it is that we, or our group, will develop an attitude of hostility and resentment. We are reinforcing specific neural pathways in our brains. With enough repetitions the anger-response becomes automatic and less conscious.

Bobby Knight is an example of a well-known individual (Knight was a basketball coach at Indiana University) who flooded so frequently that he couldn't stop, even when it cost him his job and the support of his fans.

Toxic anger, hostility, and heart disease

Anger is a coping strategy for many individuals. To the uninformed, hostility and blame appear to help them gain an edge. Blaming others seems to sidestep the nitty-gritty work of problem-solving, or help one to take center stage and generate energy when the team is in a slump. However, one of the many costs of hostility and blame is a dramatic increase in the risk for heart disease.

The identification of Type A behavior was one of the first times Western medicine acknowledged the relationship between emotions and health. Early work in this area identified four traits that were linked to heart disease: 1) ambition, 2) urgency, 3) a competitive orientation, and 4) hostility.

However, in the mid 1980s, Dr. Redford Williams, a psychiatrist and director of the Behavioral Medical Research Center at Duke University, and Drs. Margaret Chesney and Michael Hecker at Stanford Research Institute concluded that the first three characteristics associated with Type A are not risk factors. You can be busy, in a hurry, and competitive (if you can do so without hostility), and you won't increase your risk for heart disease. These researchers discovered that *the risk factor lies in a hostile reaction* to life's inevitable frustrations. Frequent, prolonged, and intense anger increases your risk for one of America's biggest killers of both men and women.

When you become angry, your body rapidly increases the amount of available energy through an increase in hormones, blood pressure, and pulse rate. Cortisol, one the hormones released during heightened anger, is a particularly troublesome chemical. It damages the cells lining the heart, and makes it more difficult for the body to calm down.

Your defense system also secretes chemicals to thicken your blood in case you are physically wounded. People who are fueled by a regular diet of hostility are quietly developing arteriosclerosis, or hardening of the arteries, in response to elevated levels of blood-thickening chemicals. I've now heard about two cases where this happened in as little as six months.

> *No matter how many times you work out at the gym or how careful you are to eat correctly, you're putting yourself at risk if you don't manage your anger effectively.*
>
> —Hendrie Weisinger, Ph.D.

As one author states, every time you get angry it's like having one-one thousandth (1/1,000) of a heart attack. This process is controlled by an ancient defense system designed to ensure you can outrun a hungry predator. However, in modern society, wild boars rarely jump out from behind a file cabinet! In today's culture, individuals have elevated levels of cortisol and adrenaline in reaction to their own inabilities to manage relatively minor emotional events. The majority of modern-day risks for heart disease are not created by the threat of physical danger, they are created by our *thinking*.

Dr. Williams and his colleagues at Duke discovered data to support his theory that hostility and heart disease are linked. They found personality tests (the Minnesota Multiphasic Personality Inventory) that had been given to college students in 1954. Twenty-five years had passed since the students had taken the test. One of the traits measured by the test was hostility. Williams suspected that if they were correct, they would find a correlation between high levels of hostility and early death rates.

Williams found that in the low hostility group, 5 percent had died during the following 25 years. However, *20* percent of the high hostility group had died, from various causes, but primarily from heart disease.

Prior to Dr. Williams's work, most researchers agreed that the main risk factors associated with heart disease were cigarette smoking, high cholesterol, and high blood pressure. However, the link between emotions and health is so powerful that in his best-selling book, *The Trusting Heart*, Dr. Williams concludes that hostility is a better predictor of death rates from coronary blockage than the other three factors.

A study at the University of North Carolina tracked medical doctors for 25 years and found the ones with high hostility scores were *seven times* more likely to die from heart disease by age 50 than those with low hostility scores.

At 100 heartbeats per minute, we can no longer hear

Dr. John Gottman, a researcher and psychologist, spent 20 years obtaining biofeedback data (heart rhythms, blood pressure, and so on) on couples while they were engaged in tense discussions. In his book, *The Seven Principles That Make Marriages Work* (Three Rivers Press, 2000), Gottman relates that the human body can go from a normal heartbeat (82 beats per minute for women and 76 for men) to 165 beats per minute when it believes it is at risk for harm. "When we wire couples up during a tense discussion you can see how physically distressing flooding is."

Gottman found that after your heartbeat goes above 100 beats per minute you literally cannot hear what the other person is saying, even if you try.

In addition to increasing the risk factor for heart disease, flooding also suppresses the immune system. Researchers found that when subjects just *imagined* someone they didn't like for five minutes, their immune systems were suppressed for six hours!

This information had a strong impact on me. Before I read these researchers' work I would get furious when I was on the freeway and somebody cut me off. I'd fume, "Who do you think you are—putting all of us in danger!? You jerk!"

Although I knew that getting angry with a reckless driver was useless in any practical way, I didn't see it as harmful. However, once I learned how damaging it was to my body, I made a commitment to change my response. Now, when someone does something dangerous, I think about the death rates associated with hostility and calm my body by saying, "Don't bother getting all worked up. Nature is going to take that person out of the gene pool!"

Males rage—and rescue—more often

Anthropologists believe that for 99.99 percent of the time we've been on the planet, people organized themselves in small clans of hunters and gatherers. Although men and women had great respect for the opposite gender, we were bound by rigid gender roles: women gathered and men hunted. These differences are still reflected in our physiology.

> *Our remarkable technological accomplishments notwithstanding, modern human beings still occupy cavemen bodies.*
>
> —Charles Stroebel, M.D.

Men, in their roles as hunters, faced many dangers. The ability to flood rapidly and intensely was an important asset to fend off physical danger and to subjugate prey.

These ancient differences help us understand why the majority of people in prison for violent crimes are males. In a study of 10,037 incidents of road rage, only 413 of the perpetrators were female. Men flood more quickly and intensely!

This increased tendency to flood also contributes to men performing the vast majority of rescue work. When it comes to physical heroism, flooding offers a significant benefit in terms of boosting speed and strength. However, not only is flooding a risk factor for heart disease, but the second price we pay when we flood is the ability to problem-solve.

Anger makes you stupid

When you are flooded, problem-solving, which occurs in the largest part of the human brain—the cortex—is severely impaired, and this has a profound impact on behavior. Have you ever been in a heated argument and been unable to think of a pointed response? Or have you blurted out an intended zinger that made no sense? Author Laurence Peter captured this dilemma when he wrote: "Speak when you're angry and you'll make the best speech you'll ever regret."

To add insult to injury, the point you were trying to make only becomes clear later on, then you think, "Why didn't I say...?" This is a good example of the medulla at work, hijacking higher systems of thought. Think about the ECG rhythms of frustration in Chapter One. When you flood, this ancient part of the brain pumps you up physically, but at the cost of your ability to problem-solve. Your body prepares to fight for survival even if the object of your hostility is an empty coffee pot in the company break room.

> *Intelligence capacity is diminished when frustration, anxiety or inner turmoil operate. Such emotional states cause incoherence in the rhythmic and electrical output of the heart, diminishing neurological efficiency. It's one of the reasons smart people can do stupid things.*
>
> —Doc Childre and Bruce Cryer,
> *From Chaos to Coherence*

On different occasions fire chiefs have approached me during seminars and told me that flooding is a serious concern in their work. Even *looking* at the fire starts activating the fight-or-flight response and impairs the chief's ability to think strategically. As a result, it's the policy of some municipalities to position the chief so his or her view of the fire is blocked, and all their information is auditory. By blocking the chief's view he or she is better able to avoid flooding and successfully engage in the critical problem analysis required.

In the past, therapists encouraged people to flood and act out their aggression in order to release anger. People with suppressed rage were encouraged to beat on pillows and yell as a means of resolution and release.

However, research done at Iowa State University by Dr. Brad Bushman concluded that venting doesn't eliminate or dampen the expression of violence; it actually makes it more likely it will occur again. Dr. Bushman wrote in the *Personality and Social Psychology Bulletin* (June, 2002), "Venting to reduce anger is like using gasoline to put out a fire—it only feeds the flame. By fueling aggressive thoughts and feelings, venting also increases aggressive responses."

In other words, it weakens people's natural inhibitions against violent outbursts and, according to HeartMath, reinforces the neurons that make this reaction automatic. In the book *Anger: The Misunderstood Emotion*, author Carol Tavris wrote, "The biggest, fattest cultural myth, the elephant in our living room...is that catharsis is good for you."

Is yelling effective?

As I presented this data during a seminar, a construction supervisor blurted out, "But you don't understand. Yelling at people works! When I yell at a contractor I get results! They move!" I was sympathetic to his frustration, as I was challenging one of his favorite motivational strategies. "John," I responded, "when you yell, they do respond to your anger. However, they are becoming physiologically flooded, and their ability to problem-solve will be impaired. Is that the kind of worker you want on your site?" John grew quiet as he weighed this important consequence of losing his temper.

June Rice-Tangney and Ronda Dearling, in the book *Shame and Guilt,* found that feelings of shame, which are usually the result of an attack on the *person*, not a specific behavior, actually provoke more anger toward others and do little, to nothing, to bring about an improvement in behavior.

When we give in to our anger and scream at partners, employees, or children they certainly scramble. But as their bodies activate flight or fight, they will be unable to fully utilize their cortex. In addition, they are going to be focused on two reactions that will be hidden: how to 1) save face and 2) get even. John will likely never discover how the contractor he yelled at saved face with his peers, be it through a cutting retort behind John's back, or an act of sabotage at the construction site. Remember, low status employees get even—in ways that are undetected by the boss. In Chapter Seven we'll explore the themes of retribution, retaliation, and revenge in detail.

The oblivious driver and the *reflexive* response

Let's take a first-person look at the link between inflammatory thinking, flooding, and behavior through the following true story.

You are running late for an important appointment with a valued customer and your anxiety is increasing as you hit a series of red lights. At one red light, you watch with irritation as the driver immediately in front of you focuses her attention on the back seat. Sure enough, when the light changes, she doesn't notice. You tap your horn impatiently, but she ignores you. You can't believe what you're seeing as she gets out of her car, opens the back door, and starts digging around in the backseat! Your heart starts to race and you look for an out, but an illegally parked delivery truck blocks the right lane. You start leaning on your horn, as you roll down your window and scream at her to move. She continues to ignore you but within one or two minutes she returns to her seat and drives away.

If you were to generate examples of blaming, inflammatory responses to this situation, they might include:

"She's an idiot and got her license in a Cracker Jack box!"

"She's putting on her make up."

"She's a welfare cheat, with nothing to do and doesn't care that other people are busy."

"She's rich and too uppity to care about others."

"She's too stupid to realize the light has changed."

"She's from Generation X and doesn't care about others."

"She's old and senile."

"She's a woman driver!"

"She's an immigrant and doesn't care about our rules."

During seminars I ask people to brainstorm examples of blame in response to this story, and the energy in the room skyrockets. People are laughing and boisterous. The energy of blame is self-righteous and indignant.

But if you analyze the list of reactions, you'll notice that all of these statements are assumptions about the *person*. She is attacked for lack of intelligence, for her character, gender, economic status (too poor or too rich), age (too young or too old), and ethnicity.

In inflammatory thinking we exaggerate the importance and severity of the other person's behavior and we typically assume that the trait is permanent. This is one of the primary reasons blaming responses don't work. They focus on people, who are unlikely or unable to change, not the problem. Consequently, we feel hopeless about finding a solution, and thus the frustration seems insurmountable and unmerited. It's this *approach* to solving the problem that causes you to flood, not the problem itself.

I'm frustrated and it's *my* fault

Sometimes when we are frustrated, instead of blaming others we turn contempt inward and blame ourselves (Figure 5). This reaction is less visible. Most people publicly blame others, but privately berate themselves. However, depression comes from the same thinking pattern as hostility toward others—the arrow of blame just swings *inward*.

If you're stuck behind someone who's behaving in a seemingly irrational way and doesn't proceed when the light changes, you might initially react reflexively—with blame. However, later in the day, when the adrenaline and cortisol fade, your critical voices shred your self-esteem. In this thinking pattern, responses might be similar to: "Boy, I really lost it back there. I'm such a mindless jerk for getting angry over something so minor. My client was delayed too and she didn't even realize I was late." Or "Jeez, I hope no one saw me screaming at the lady. I must have looked like that idiot on TV who punched the elderly driver. I'm such a loser."

Some individuals resort to self-contempt immediately upon becoming frustrated. "Why did I take this stupid route? I should have taken the expressway! I can't even drive to an appointment without getting behind some freaking, stuck car. My stupid luck."

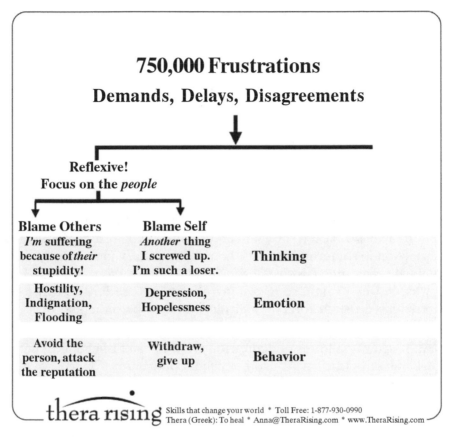

Figure 5. Frustration: arrow to blame self

Depression, work, and health

Like hostility, depression has negative effects on health and productivity. A study by Geisinger Health Systems in Pennsylvania, published in the *Journal of the American Medical Association* (June 18, 2003), found approximately 9 percent of the workforce is affected by depression at any given time, but it is often invisible to bosses and coworkers. Depressed employees report losing more than five hours per week from reduced performance due to fatigue, irritability, and loss of focus. A study at Columbia University estimated that one in five adolescents—the workers of the future—are seriously depressed. Suicides within this age group have tripled since 1995.

Depression is considered a significant risk factor for heart disease in both men and women, and depression's toll on the body also translates into a sluggish immune system. Not only are depressed people more susceptible to colds and viruses, new studies on the immune system show that depression is a risk factor for cancer.

Our bodies produce approximately 200 imperfect cells a day. These cells are missing two characteristics. They do not have an identity, so the cell doesn't become functioning part of the brain, bone, and so on, and they are missing a cap that says, "Stop reproducing, you're complete." Because of these flaws, these imperfect cells have the potential to develop into cancer.

However, a normal immune system will scan for these imperfect cells and destroy them. When the immune system is impaired by depression, this function is compromised and the risk for cancer increases. Not everyone who is depressed will get cancer, and not everyone who has cancer was depressed (there are many cancer antecedents); however, depression is a risk factor, and individuals should be screened for it and treated.

Although some forms of depression are the result of chemical imbalance, harsh self-criticism is the other major contributor. Clearly, we need to help individuals access the tools that bring relief.

Contemplate this data: Cancer and heart disease are the two biggest killers in modern society, and you can substantially lower your risk for both of these diseases by paying attention to *how you think* when you face frustration.

The stinky twins: Blaming others and blaming self

Without awareness of these negative consequences, it is easy for blaming responses to become habitual reactions to frustration.

Contempt vacillates between blaming others (B.O.), which results in feelings of hostility, to blaming self (B.S.), which results in self-loathing and depression. I call blaming others and blaming self the stinky twins. They are twins because they consist of the same DNA, or thinking patterns: "I'm frustrated because of *someone's* stupidity!" The only difference between B.O. and B.S. is the target of the blame. In B.O. the target is another person and in B.S. the target is ourselves.

I call the twins "stinky" because, frankly, they stink! These two responses to frustration damage our relationships, health, momentum, and mood, *and* they are 100 percent ineffective in solving problems. Hence, problems accumulate, weigh us down, and lead to feelings of hopelessness and frustration.

Blaming others, which is anchored at the left end of the continuum, results in anger and the energy of hostility. Blaming self, which is anchored in the middle of the continuum, results in loss of energy, or depression.

Targeting someone else is a quick antidote to harsh self-criticism. Pay attention to what highly critical people say when they make a mistake—their *self*-evaluations are chilling. They'll say things such as, "I'm so stupid! What an idiot! That's just like me! I'll never get this right!"

When you aim anger and hostility toward another person, you have energy. It may not feel good, but it's preferable to *not* having energy. Watch for this in your moments of frustration. Do you vacillate between being angry and critical of others, and berating yourself? When you feel contempt for others, it may be in order to relieve the despair that accompanies self-loathing.

> *B.O. and B.S. were somewhat the same*
> *Each one adept at resorting to blame*
> *B.O. pointed fingers to preserve a good name*
> *B.S. wrung hands in guilt and then shame.*

> —Nancy Clemens, NJ Clemens & Associates, Inc.

Once again, imagine the accumulated effect of these two thinking patterns over time. Remember, an average of 30 frustrations per day results in more than 750,000 in a lifetime! This level of frequency allows for plenty of opportunities to fall into invisible but counterproductive habits.

The flooded boss

To see how outer and inner blame are linked, imagine I'm a vice president who knows nothing about flooding and its dire consequences. I flood frequently—after all, once in awhile I *deserve* an outburst! I've earned it and you're not going to deny me my rights to express my indignation about sloppy work! I shouldn't have to put up with ineffi-ciencies and laziness!

During a hectic day, when nerves are frayed, one of my direct re-ports, Megan, warily tells me that her presentation to the executive team will have to be rescheduled because of problems in the database. I ex-plode and tell her I've just about had it with her poor planning! Even if Megan's been warned about my "hot temper," she will be insulted and hurt by my tirade. However, because of my ability to problem-solve and listen is impaired, I will be in no condition to care about Megan's feelings or notice her reactions.

My tirade carries a big, hidden price. My irrational response will de-stroy her willingness to exceed my expectations for the sheer pleasure of pleasing someone she respects and trusts. Her passion, her opinion of me, and her pride in work are now at risk.

However, even more damage will result as a consequence of my self-righteous behavior. If I tend to vacillate between blaming others and blaming myself, after the cortisol and adrenaline fade, I will turn my contempt and inflammatory thinking on myself in the form of harsh self-criticism: "I'm such a lousy supervisor. Why did I say that? This is MY fault; she's only been here six months and I knew this assignment was a stretch for her. I should have paid more attention to her progress. I hope she doesn't resign—I'd hate to lose another direct report this year. I'm lousy at supervising people. I never should have taken this promotion. I never know when to let well enough alone."

Blaming has turned on me. Now I feel terrible *and* I've lost my energy. Of the three reactions to frustration, this is the worst. What's the quickest way to regain it? Blame someone! I can turn the arrow of blame toward the Information Technology department or the person responsible for that particular database. Pumped out with renewed self-righteous indignation I stop the IT director in the hall, and make poorly informed accusations against his group, which angers the director and his staff. I might feel terrible, but now I have energy!

Ha! I could even use my anger toward them as a way of soothing over the situation with Megan. I could apologize to her and tell her the prob-lem is really the incompetence of the IT group. Although she might buy my contriteness and feel relieved that she is no longer a target of my contempt, at a deeper, unexpressed level she will no longer trust me.

The most tragic outcome of swinging back and forth between inner and outer blame is that the resulting isolation, hostility and self-criticism will keep me from focusing on the problem—the database is inaccurate. However, I have alienated the very people, including the IT department and Megan, both of whom I need in order to solve the problem.

In addition, my hostile attacks will damage her morale and self-confidence, making it more difficult for her to learn or solve the problem. She'll tell others about my hostile reaction and they will be empathic to her embarrassment by telling her *their* stories about run-ins with me.

At some level I know that I am the topic of office gossip. Now I am even more vulnerable to depression, and its twin, aggression. Why is the organization turning against *me*?!

Hostility and the fear of unworthiness

What causes hostility? Although many factors come into play, Dr. Williams (page 49) concluded that cynicism, or a general mistrust of other people's motives, fuels hostility.

Cynicism is not skepticism. Skepticism is occasional doubt and concerns specific individuals. Cynicism is negativity across the board, and applies to every situation and every person. It's the attitude, "I don't trust anyone but you and me, Dick, and I'm starting to worry about you!" It's contempt *before* investigation.

What causes cynicism? Think of the most cynical person you know. Does fragile self-esteem fit? Anger and cynicism help individuals fend off threats to their sense of self-worth.

James Gilligam, M.D., author of *Violence: Our Deadly Epidemic and Its Causes*, has never seen a serious act of violence that was not "provoked by the experience of feeling shamed and humiliated, disrespected and ridiculed." The United States Secret Service interviewed 40 boys involved in school shootings and found that many of them were persistently humiliated and harassed over long periods.

Rudeness and incivility have a toxic effect on individuals at work and in society at large because they are perceived as an attack on one's identity, self-concept, or status. Consequently, individuals react with anger and a desire for revenge that is disproportionate to the triggering behavior.

Hostility appears to be a smoke screen behind which people hide their feelings of unworthiness, avoid feelings of worthlessness, and defend their identities.

Naomi Eisenberger, of the University of California, Los Angeles, has found that social rejection affects the same region of the brain as physical injuries. Just as animals in pain respond aggressively, people in emotional distress lash out with angry outbursts.

Professor Jennifer Crocker at the University of Michigan, Ann Arbor, has found that people who score high on self-esteem tests, but have unstable and *inflated* feelings of self-worth (not grounded in objective measures), are the most likely to become hostile, defensive, and aggressive when they are challenged or disappointed.

Individuals with contingent, or fragile, self-esteem base their feelings of worthiness on other people's opinions, and the success or failure of their efforts, moment to moment. Even though their esteem scores may score at average or above, when disappointed or confronted, they react with aggression, even violent aggression. Hostility can be a reaction to an extreme, underlying fear that others will judge them worthless. Hence, people with unstable self-esteem easily become defensive, unsupportive, and non-empathic.

> *Nastiness can be a mask for a person's insecurities.*
> *Kindness penetrates that.*
>
> —Judy Orloff, M.D.

Imagine you have a very cynical direct report, Beatrice, who always complains about change. As you arrive at work, she is ranting about a new software program.

If you decide that she is unappreciative of what it takes to stay in business, you will mirror her negativity and feel annoyed and impatient. Your attitude toward her will be quite obvious even if you try to hide it.

However, if you consider that her complaints might be due to lack of confidence or anxiety about not measuring up, your attitude might shift. Your reaction might be similar to, "Come on Beatrice, download the program and I'll walk you through the changes."

In dealing with defensive and blaming clients, I always make the assumption that self-esteem is the core of issue. I assume that this person is attempting to defend their sense of self. This thought keeps me from getting hooked by their contempt. Instead, I respond to their predicament with warmth. As you'll see later, if your goal is to bring about change, and not judge what is "right," kindness is much more effective than contempt.

The Rabbi and the Grand Dragon of the KKK

After I read Dr. Williams's and Dr. Crocker's work about the relationship between self-esteem and aggression I not only changed my approach to dealing with hostile employees, I began to look for examples of the link between fragile, unstable self-esteem, and hostility.

There is an extraordinary example of this relationship between self-loathing and hostility in the true story of Larry Trapp, the former Grand Dragon of the White Knights of the Ku Klux Klan of Nebraska, and the Weisser family, who befriended him. This story, about a duel between positive and negative energy, is one of the most enlightening chronicles of the last century. It's the basis of Kathryn Watterson's award-winning book, *Not by the Sword.* If we are serious about reducing the amount of hostility in our world and workplaces, the Weisser story is loaded with insight.

Larry Trapp was an example of someone at the far left end of the hostility continuum introduced in Chapter One. As Grand Dragon, Larry spent his days sending out hate mail, sponsoring racist videos on cable TV, and organizing and encouraging fellow Klansmen (and other white suprema-

cists) to target, harm, and terrorize blacks, Jews, Asians, Hispanics, Indians, and gays and lesbians, particularly in Lincoln, Nebraska, and surrounding areas.

One of the families Larry Trapp terrorized was that of the local cantor and acting rabbi, Michael Weisser, and his wife, Julie. Larry called their house and threatened, "You'll be sorry you ever

Figure 6. Trapp in regalia
Used with permission from Kathryn Watterson

moved into 5800 Randolph Street, Jew boy." He sent hate mail and a note: "The KKK Is Watching YOU."

Michael and Julie are examples of individuals at the right end of the continuum—individuals whose warmth and skill combine in an extraordinary ability to transform destructive behavior.

Larry's first hate-filled call to the Weisser household shocked and angered Michael and Julie. But Michael was used to confronting prejudice and hostility in his work as spiritual leader of his synagogue. Michael's anger gradually turned to curiosity, and later to concern.

Michael began calling Larry and leaving messages that were meant to make Larry think about how irrational it is to build a worldview based on hatred and blame. Knowing that Larry was suffering from diabetes and confined to a wheelchair, Michael would confront Larry with, "I don't know why you worship Hitler, you would have been one of the first people he would have killed."

Sometimes his messages were from Michael's heart, "Larry, if you ever get tired of hating, there's a whole world of love waiting for you."

Over time, Michael and Julie tempered their conversations with warmth and offers of help. Larry's attitude shifted slightly. He wasn't used to warmth and kindness. It disarmed him.

After months of emotional phone calls, Michael received a call that was unlike any other. Larry said bluntly, "I want to get out, but I don't know how." Larry was beginning to recognize the link between hostility and health. "I'm feeling confused and kind of sick. I think this is making me sick." Michael asked if Larry wanted to talk and, surprisingly, Larry acquiesced.

When Julie and Michael arrived at Larry's apartment, they were surprised and saddened by the reality of what lay behind the smokescreen of hostility. Larry was an unkempt, disheveled man, who had lost both of his lower legs to diabetes and was going blind. He was sitting alone in a barren, dirty apartment surrounded by guns, hate literature, bomb-making supplies, and Nazi and Klan paraphernalia.

Larry's rage kept introspection and depression at bay.

—Kathryn Watterson, *Not by the Sword*

Michael reached out to shake hands with Larry, and Larry began to sob. Underneath his misdirected rage, Larry was exhausted and feeling hopeless about his barren life. His misery and isolation had been exacerbated by the energy he was investing in targeting and harassing others, and, more importantly, it was blocking him from creating positive relationships with people who might befriend him.

Larry apologized repeatedly for his history of terrorizing and hurting others. The next day, at great risk to his own safety, Larry renounced his membership and asked other Klan members to do the same. He then began a long process of reaching out to people he had harassed and asking for their forgiveness.

The local paper ran an article on the Trapp/Weisser story, which was picked up by the Associated Press, the *New York Times,* and *Time* magazine. Julie and Michael quietly continued to bring Larry meals and medicine, and transport him to the doctor.

After months of trips between the two homes, it became clear that Larry was dying. Julie decided it would be much easier to care for him if he lived in their home. One of the Weisser's adolescent daughters moved into the basement and Larry took up residence in her former room.

In response to this loving family, Larry thrived. Eventually, he asked Michael to teach him Hebrew. Before he died, Larry converted to Judaism.

Figure 7. Larry Trapp and Weisser Family

Hostility brings relief from self-loathing

One of the most disturbing, yet revealing aspects of the Weisser/ Trapp story occurred just before Larry's death. During his Klan days Larry claimed he hated African-Americans because he had been gang-raped by a group of black adolescents at reform school. However, his last confession to Julie, the one that was the most difficult for him to make, was that he hadn't been raped. As a young man he had consensual sex with a black male. Larry, who had been raised with intolerance and contempt, judged himself mercilessly and turned his inner hostility into outer hatred for the sheer relief from self-loathing. This is a classic example of the cycle we discussed in the early pages of this chapter; the thinking patterns of "blame others" and "blame self" are linked. Again, we are watching someone trying to preserve a fragile sense of *worthiness.*

Shame, which is a condemnation of the person, rather than the behavior, is more likely to provoke anger toward others than change the offending behavior. Larry's story provides a rare opportunity to see extreme hostility for what it is: an attempt to escape unbearable criticism of self. Like most people who get caught in this trap, Larry became increasingly anxious and depressed as he discovered that targeting and despising other people wasn't bringing him what they need most: respect and peace of mind.

When Larry met the Weissers, he was at a turning point. His deteriorating health made it undeniably clear—he didn't have much time left to get it right. When Julie and Michael offered their sincere friendship, Larry dropped his hostility in a heartbeat for an opportunity to be loved.

Hostility collapses into hopelessness and despair

On a much less dramatic scale, I have seen this exact dynamic many times while working with teams that are incapacitated by internal hostility and conflict. When I come into an organization to resolve conflict, team members are eager to cooperate. Their initial rush of hostility has withered into a black hole of despair. Team members are exhausted from tension, and they ache for positive interactions and the respect of their supervisors and peers.

When hostility is used as a primary means of generating passion, it robs individuals, such as Larry, of their primary desire—achievement and camaraderie. In later chapters we'll explore this in depth.

Without positive energy, two dismal choices remain

There are only three options for energy: to have none (depression or indifference), to generate energy through hostility, or to build it through appreciation and achievement. When we fail to provide the conditions that create positive energy, or when we lack the skills to generate it, employees are left with two dismal choices. They either function *without* workplace energy, disconnected from the mission, and each other; or they target others as a means of stimulation and as a way in which to bond with members of their in-group. However, depression is so debilitating that it is the *least* preferred state, and therefore most groups facing this choice unconsciously gravitate to the energy of hostility.

Employees who work in isolation are vulnerable to hostility because individuals will do almost anything to escape tedium. In fact, isolation is so punishing that solitary confinement is used as a deterrent in prisons. In low-stimulus settings people are forced to make a choice between being energized by contempt and not being energized at all (the first and second columns of "Three Cultures at Work," page 32). When we are forced to choose between these two alternatives, we would rather have the stimulation of hostility than experience the under-arousal of depression.

This has been borne out in studies of security guards. To avoid facing a night of mind-numbing boredom, security workers create energy by playing nasty practical jokes, gossiping, and committing minor acts of sabotage.

In my work, I have yet to find anyone who *desired* to be energized by hostility. However, as Albert Einstein concluded, the energy of hostility can be created by anyone, while creating the energy of appreciation takes conscious commitment, skill, and courage.

When leaders believe that creating climates of appreciation isn't a priority or worth their time, I ask them which of the other two choices they'd prefer. Do they want their employees to create the energy of hostility by using gossip and ridicule to enliven an otherwise tedious day? Or do they want employees to stop seeking energy from work, and withdraw and disengage from the organization's mission? This question always causes even the most die-hard skeptics to rethink their position.

In addition, if you're a formal or informal leader, I have very bad news. Because leaders are visible and their role requires they make unpopular decisions, they are among *the* most frequent targets of blame.

When managers tolerate blame, they also become targets as their employees mirror their tendency to assume that every frustration is the result of a thoughtless clod.

If blame becomes the sugar high of your work group or organization, regardless of your competence and character, *you* will most certainly be one of many people whom your group targets in your absence.

Sending the stinky twins to reform school

There is a third, superb, and life-sustaining option. In the next chapter we'll focus on the situation-based, problem-solving response to frustration, return to the story of the oblivious driver, and examine the impact of positive emotions on health, relationships, and effectiveness. Here you will find an abundance of good news. You'll also discover that when you lose interest in blaming others/blaming self, you'll make a dramatic shift toward better health, feelings of well-being, effectiveness, and self-confidence.

During seminars, individuals are riveted to the information about flooding, the medulla, cortex, heart disease, and inner and outer contempt. However, there is a palpable sense of relief as we turn our attention to the *positive* thinking patterns that sustain individuals, protect health, motivate groups, and maximize accomplishments.

Although we are mesmerized by climates of fear, ridicule, and defensiveness, they cannot sustain us. For optimal, long-term performance, we must be in environments where our energy can be continuously renewed.

Our longings for positive workplaces are reliable and ancient, for it is within healthy communities that we realize our best health, creativity, and achievements.

> *"I don't know what to say," Larry said between more tears. "I've been so terrible to you and to so many people. I can't believe I hated you so much. How can you ever forgive me?"*
>
> *"We do forgive you," Julie said. "We do."*
>
> *"I don't know what, but I...I just feel different." Larry said, putting the palm of his hand on his stomach. "I've never felt like this before."*
>
> —Kathryn Watterson, *Not by the Sword*

Chapter Three

Curiosity Makes You Smart, Sexy, and Successful: The Most Important Habit You Bring to the Table

The arrival of a good clown exercises a more beneficial influence upon the health of a town than the arrival of twenty asses laded with drugs.
                    —John Sydenham, 17th-century physician

Well, okay, maybe reflective reactions don't really make us sexy, but they do make us more effective, knowledgeable, and respected. Giving people the benefit of the doubt when things aren't going well and resisting the urge to flood endears us to others.

In contrast, people who use the blaming response covered in Chapter Two assume an incompetent, immoral, or insensitive *person* lies at the root of their distress, and their irrational, destructive responses erode their reputations and integrity.

When we use the *reflexive* response, we assume someone else's characteristics are the cause of *our* discomfort. We scan their personality, age, ethnicity, gender, occupation, and so on, to pinpoint their responsibility in our frustration. It's as if we are saying, "WHOSE fault is this? A mindless idiot is making my life miserable!"

This reaction is common when people feel overwhelmed. However, it is paralyzing and destructive. In addition to the health risks covered in Chapter Two, reflexive reactions impair our ability to solve problems in any meaningful way. Because we assume the problem lies within some-one else's characteristics, we feel as if we are powerless victims without solutions. No wonder this thinking pattern causes flooding!

In contrast, when we use the situational-orientation (Figure 8) we search the *situation* for the source of the problem. "WHAT is causing their behavior? What could be going on?" In this response, we assume that the other person is *reasonable*, and once we know the whole story, his or her behavior will make sense. We may not agree with the other person's actions, but we assume that the other party is responding to something in his or her environment that we are unaware of. This as-sumption shapes the manner in which we approach the individual and our chances for success.

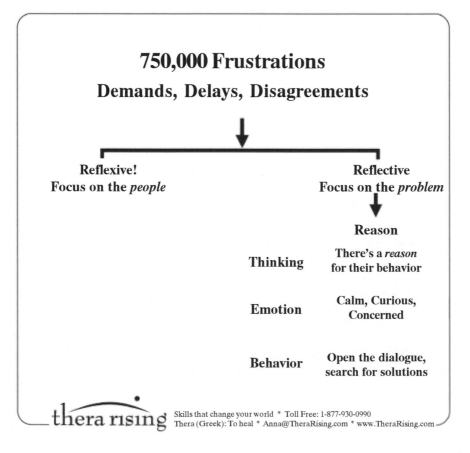

Figure 8: Frustration: arrow to reason

When we engage in *reflective* thinking we utilize the **cortex**, the problem-solving center of the brain. Reflective thinking is more rational and less volatile. It considers options and possibilities. Rather than feeling indignant, we become *curious* about the reasons for the other party's behavior. This attitude brings us closer to the heart rhythms of appreciation from Chapter One, which is associated with increased creativity and mental clarity.

Instead of attacking the competence and character of others, or withdrawing to avoid confrontation, a reflective stance leads us to seek out the other party, open the dialogue, and ask for his or her assistance in understanding. This reaction has multiple benefits to physical health, effectiveness, mood, and the ability to maintain relationships.

Roosevelt: Reflective, analytical, and effective

Franklin Roosevelt is a well-known political leader who faced a staggering economic crisis, but approached it with a radically different approach than his nemesis in Europe, Hitler. Roosevelt looked at the situation as a problem with the financial regulations underlying the banking industry and stock market. As a result, he passed more legislation in his first 100 days in office than any president before him.

Roosevelt and Hitler give us a dramatic snapshot of the impact of these two thinking patterns; blaming people versus looking to the situation, structures, pressures, and limitations as the source of problems. (See Figure 9 on page 70).

Let's return to the true story from Chapter Two about Tony, and his boss's decision to move the plant to South Carolina. After the surprise announcement, most of Tony's colleagues went on a "search for stupidity" about whom to blame for the relocation. Their bodies were flooded with cortisol and adrenaline, and their thinking was dominated by self-righteousness. However, this reaction destroys their ability to problem-solve. In addition, as they alienated the people they targeted (engineering, marketing, the owner), their reactions damaged the relationships they needed to regain momentum and address the problem—by beginning their search to find new employment.

Contrast their *reflexive*, personality-based reactions with Tony's calm, *reflective* response. After making the rounds to various departments, Tony went back to his office, closed the door, updated his resume, and wrote

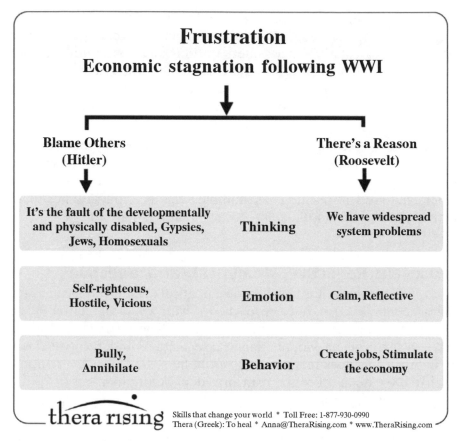

Figure 9. Frustration: Roosevelt and Hitler

several cover letters. About an hour later he went out to chat with his legal assistant and realized his colleagues were still clustered about, complaining angrily about the sudden turn of events. He was dumbfounded that they were wasting precious time, instead of getting down to task.

The contrast of Tony's reaction to those of his colleagues can be explained by Tony's thinking. Instead of "awfulizing," he accepted the corporate closing as an unfortunate, but not catastrophic, event. Instead of blaming the president or other departments, Tony assumed the owner had substantial reasons to move his company to another part of the country.

In fact, within a year of the move, Tony learned that his former boss had died from cancer. Although Tony was unable to confirm it, he suspected that the president returned home in anticipation of his declining health. While many of Tony's colleagues assumed that the cause of the closing was someone's fault—engineering, marketing, the boss—Tony assumed there was a reason, albeit, hidden. This assumption allowed him to stay calm, relaxed, and focused on task. It also allowed him to maintain relationships that he otherwise would have lost needlessly.

Tony's ability to stay composed and effective was the result of his ability to look at the *situation* as the source of the problem, not various people. His superb control over his reactions to frustration and his automatic responses allowed him to optimize an unexpected, negative event. Tony maintained his momentum, relationships, and effectiveness during a period that others found debilitating.

Let's return to another previous example, that of Rhonda, the anxious VP of sales. If she uses a situational-orientation, she will assume the problem lies in the organization's systems or processes. Rather than starting a rumor about Ted, the VP of operations, and attacking his competence, Rhonda will move in the opposite direction, and approach Ted directly to learn about his constraints. In fact, she will look for ways to help Ted out of his predicament. As you'll see in Chapter Six, the odds are on our side when we make the assumption that workplace problems really reflect problems in systems, roles, or inadequate information.

This reaction has multiple benefits. By sidestepping the opportunity to promote herself at Ted's expense, Rhonda won't get ensnared in a debilitating power struggle with Ted. In addition, by learning about Ted's constraints and gathering data, she may be able to minimize the impact of the backlog on her group. Helping Ted resolve his productivity issues rather than personally benefiting from his problems—at the expense of their organization's profitability—will send a significant signal to her peers about her character. If Rhonda and Ted look for problems in the context of work rather than personalities, they will most likely uncover system problems that they then will have the opportunity to resolve.

Ted will be relieved and grateful if Rhonda *doesn't* use his department's crisis as an opportunity to increase her status. Ted will be very likely to reciprocate her professionalism at a later date when Rhonda's group misses a quota or experiences a shortfall. It is these kinds of positive reactions to a crisis that bond workers to each other, and make work exciting, energizing, and meaningful.

The oblivious driver and the reflective reaction

Let's also return to the true story of the "oblivious driver" and contrast the reflective, or problem-solving, reaction to the blame reactions we used earlier. In the personality-based reactions, you assumed the woman who wasn't moving after the light changed was too stupid or selfish to care about anyone but herself.

If, instead, you use a reflective, situational-based approach when the woman opens the back door of her vehicle, you'll assume there's a *reason* why she's focused on the backseat.

If you speculate that the unyielding driver has a legitimate *motive* for her behavior (in contrast to an inflammatory, personality-based approach) you will be able to avoid flooding with anger and adrenaline. It's likely you won't shift into the medulla, the fight-or-flight center of the brain. Instead, you'll utilize the cortex, the source of creativity and problem-solving.

Thinking reflectively, from the cortex, allows situational possibilities to surface. It's similar to asking, "Why would a *reasonable* person have her attention on the back seat rather than driving?" The possibilities are limitless:

> The pizza fell on the floor.
>
> She's lost and her map is in the back of her car.
>
> A baby needs a bottle.
>
> She has asthma (or diabetes) and she's looking for her medication.
>
> She flicked a cigarette out the window, it blew back in, and it's burning the backseat.
>
> She's tending to an elderly person who's ill.

During a seminar, when people switch from personality-based thinking to a situational-orientation, they stop ridiculing the driver and joking at her expense. They become more reflective and concerned, and I watch the influence of the cortex on their behavior. Individuals become empathic and start telling stories about similar experiences from their own lives. The energy created in this reflective mood is dramatically different than the self-righteous, aggressive energy of blame. This thinking pattern engenders compassion and a desire to be of assistance, rather than contempt.

"BIBS"

As I mentioned earlier, the example of the "oblivious driver" is based on a true story. The driver who was focused on the backseat of her car wrote a letter to the editor of the local paper because she was determined to tell her side of the story

The reason she didn't move her vehicle when the light changed was because her toddler, who was riding in the backseat, was choking! In her letter she explained the man behind her had flooded and began blowing his horn as she frantically tried to clear her toddler's throat. Of course she ignored the green light. Any frantic parent would behave in a similar manner.

Her experience is a perfect example of the deficits of a personality-based approach and the kind of emotions and behavior it elicits. *When we are flooded with hostility, we are not only useless, we often make the problem worse.*

In Chapter Four there are additional stories of hidden realities, similar to this one. I call hidden realities "babies in the backseat." In the workplace, hidden realities can be materials shortages, lack of information, process problems, budget cuts, union constraints, safety restrictions, and so on.

An easy way to remember the three assumptions is that the reflexive reactions are the stinky twins, B.O. and B.S., and the reflective response is BIBS or "baby in the back seat." These terms are used as lighthearted, shorthand messages, or code within teams and organizations.

More than once a CEO has told me that he uses the phrase, "baby in the back seat" to avoid flooding or shooting the messenger. The term will help you remember to look for *why*, rather than *who*.

When teams and individuals face a crisis, it's not the amount of external stress that distinguishes healthy organizations from toxic ones. It's not the business climate, profitability, the competition, or the severity of the predicament. I've consulted in organizations that were enjoying tremendous profits but were unable to retain their people because their climates were riddled with blame. I've also been in organizations where they were literally closing facilities, and yet former employees had nothing but good things to say about the way they were treated and the reasons their facility closed.

The pivotal difference lies in the organization's cultural response to frustration. If your organization or team is able to face aggravations without blaming others, you'll pull together during stressful times and optimize your opportunities.

If you or your team resort to reflexive, inflammatory responses, and assume that every inconvenience is proof of another party's incompetence, then even minor events will trigger blame and mistrust, and generate competing, negative factions. You will alienate other departments, and waste valuable assets on power struggles and mistrust.

Later we'll look at these responses in more detail, but I want to return to the discussion about emotions and health. If hostility and depression have negative impacts on health, does appreciation have a positive effect? If it does, organizations would be wise to promote it.

The health and happiness benefits of appreciation and affection

As we saw in Chapter Two, hostility gives us a "sugar high" of energy, but it comes with a hefty price tag of diminished health. Anger is a significant risk factor for heart disease. Blame leads to social isolation, which often results in depression. We also know that isolation and depression carry health risks. Fortunately, at the positive end of the continuum where we placed feelings of affection or love, the data about impact on health is extremely heartening. Larry Dossey, M.D., puts it succinctly, "Love is intimately related to health."

Dr. Gregory Berns, a psychiatrist at Emory University in Atlanta, conducted research by using magnetic resonance imaging and found that when participants cooperated while playing a laboratory game, the mental circuitry normally associated with reward-seeking behavior became active. In other words, cooperation feels *good*.

Feelings of affection occur when we are part of a tightly knit group, bonded by loyalty and fun. This end of the continuum includes the joy of accomplishment; love for family members; faith and spiritual practices; and respect and appreciation for colleagues, mentors, and supervisors. Additionally, satisfaction from a customer, the joy of recognition, feelings of camaraderie, and the satisfaction of helping others achieve their goals also fall into this end of the spectrum.

Love and health

You probably know individuals who are energized by love. Their faces become more beautiful, even as their bodies age. It lends another interpretation to Coco Chanel's phrase, "By the time you're 50 you have the face you deserve." Her observation is true not only for people whose lives are consumed by hostility and cynicism, but also for people who thrive on love and appreciation.

Although there is less research in the area of health and love than in the field of health and hostility, interesting data is accumulating. For instance, researchers scanning emergency room data discovered that heart attack victims who arrived at the hospital with family or friends were three times more likely to survive than people who came in alone.

In a study by Stanford University psychiatrist David Spiegel (reported in May, 1989, at the American Psychiatric Association meeting), women with terminal breast cancer were divided into two groups. One of the groups met twice a week to talk about their fears, and receive support from other patients. In the final stages of the disease, they developed into a tightly knit community and their friendships extended beyond their scheduled meetings.

Spiegel waited two years to analyze his final data and said, "I almost fell off my chair when I read the study's outcomes." The group that developed an intense connection lived twice as long as the group without support. A small, nonchemical intervention had significantly prolonged the lives of the women in the support groups. Being in community not only elevates our mood, it has a measurable impact on our bodies.

Caring is biological.

—Dr. James Lynch,
University of Maryland School of Medicine

Another surprise finding occurred when researchers were testing rabbits for the potency of arteriosclerosis drugs. Although all the rabbits were subjected to high-fat diets, the ones that received daily petting from a kindhearted laboratory technician had significantly lower levels of the disease.

Affection and the immune system

Remember the experiment from Chapter Two, where hostility negatively affected immune systems? The same researchers also asked students to focus for five minutes on someone they loved, or a peak experience. Their immune systems functioned at a higher level for *six hours* after five minutes of relaxing into the energy of appreciation. If this dramatic impact on the immune system is found with people who are just *remembering* a hostile or positive experience, imagine the impact when we are experiencing these events in real life!

Ever since I learned about this research finding, I've adopted a ritual. In the morning, before I get out of bed, and at night, before I fall asleep, I consciously think of someone I love, or things for which I am grateful. These two, five-minute periods in combination boost my immune system for a total of 12 hours! It feels *wonderful*, and during a Minnesota winter, generating feelings of appreciation is as easy as thinking about the thermostat for the furnace that automatically turns up the heat before I get out of bed. I also gained an unexpected return. I began to feel the energy of appreciation throughout the day. I used to struggle with frequent head colds that lasted for months, but since I adopted this practice six or seven years ago I've only had two colds and they disappeared within a few days. I attribute my increased immunity to this simple practice.

This assumption was confirmed by an experiment conducted at the University of Pittsburg. Volunteers allowed the researchers to place a cold virus in their nostrils. Individuals who described themselves as "happy and relaxed" came down with colds at one-third the rate of people who were the least likely to use those words.

The helper's high

Allan Luks, the director of Big Brothers Big Sisters of New York, teamed up with Howard Andrews, a biopsychologist, to investigate the effect of volunteer work on health. They found that people who volunteer on a regular basis experienced an increase in endorphins, the body's pleasure chemical. Luks dubbed this the "helper's high." It's very similar to the runner's high, except with an additional advantage. At the end of a long run, endorphins drop rapidly, resulting in a slide toward fatigue. However, with the helper's high, according to Luks, there are "long-lasting feelings of euphoria, followed by relief from symptoms like lupus and arthritis."

Luks also found that although people have the biggest endorphin reaction when they do volunteer work, he also found health is positively affected by simple acts of kindness, such as pitching in to help a colleague meet a deadline. I think about this physiological reaction as nature's message: do more of this. It enhances survival, feelings of well-being, and health. Our bodies are "wired" to feel the best when we are in positive energy.

The following short story, written by Elaine Gale of *The Minneapolis Star Tribune*, beautifully portrays how a small act of kindness has the power to change our mood.

Help across a two-way street

I stepped off the bus on my way home from work, brow furrowed, smothering under snow and seasonal obligations. The pressure of the holidays had sunk my mood.

Glaring at the pod of riders clamoring to get on the bus I had just exited, I ran into an elderly woman whose boot had stuck in a chunk of ice. Off-balance and scared, she looked up from under her green hat and asked plaintively, "Will you help me?"

"Of course!" I said, and took her arm, freed her boot, escorted her through the throng, over the icy sidewalk and across the steep drifts to the corner. Then, safely across the street, she touched my arm and said, "Thank you for your help."

Her words should have been mine. The opportunity to help her had thawed my reserve and warmed my spirit. She'd asked for my help, but it turned out I'd needed hers too.

Wealth and well-being: John D. Rockefeller

The following story about John D. Rockefeller, Sr., is another vivid example of the impact of positive and negative energy on health.

Rockefeller worked relentlessly until his early 30s, when he earned his first million. Ten years later he was at the head of the world's largest business, and became a billionaire at age 53.

However, Rockefeller's business practices were so ruthless that he made many enemies during his quest for extreme wealth. Oil field workers hanged him in effigy and he was in such fear of his life that he needed full-time bodyguards. Rockefeller could barely eat or sleep. He developed alopecia, a condition that results in the loss of body hair. He was so weak that his doctors predicted he'd only live another year.

Then, perhaps because of dismal forecasts for his health, he began to give his money away. Through the Rockefeller Foundation, he funded hospitals, universities, and missions. He used his wealth for research that led to cures for tuberculosis, malaria, diphtheria, and hookworm.

As his life became more altruistic, Rockefeller's health improved. He was able to reestablish healthy patterns of eating and sleeping, and regained his vitality. He continued his legacy of philanthropy until he died at the age of 98.

Our most elevated moods occur in relationships of affection and emotional safety, and we are intrinsically motivated to seek out feelings of well-being through acts of kindness. Consequently, I have found the most miserable people in the workplace are those who are cut off from the feelings of camaraderie through conflict or isolation.

Once you train your mind to generate feelings of appreciation, it will affect your relationships, mood, and effectiveness, regardless of your circumstances. You can generate these feelings on a crowded airplane, during a tense meeting with a vendor, or backed up in traffic. As you'll see in Chapter Nine, it won't make you less effective; it will make you *more* so. Once you "wire" your brain to avoid flooding and hostility, and see the world through the lens of abundance, the benefits will spill over to strangers, colleagues, and customers.

I call the ability to do this, "riding the wave of appreciation." Like Bruce, the Vietnam Veteran at the beginning of Chapter Two, you will be able to create feelings of serenity at will.

While I was consulting at a metropolitan law firm I'd stop at a snack shop for my morning cup of coffee. The little shop was always jammed with workers grabbing their morning beverage and racing to beat the clock. The gaunt, tattooed man behind the counter handled each customer with military efficiency, but without making the briefest eye contact or displaying the smallest gesture of warmth. As I waited in line I'd always try to notice something about him on which I could give him a positive comment as he rang up my purchase.

One morning he said to me gruffly, "You're *always* in a good mood. What's *wrong* with you?"

I laughed, but I *feel* what he noticed—I'm almost always in a good mood, and I understand how this can be puzzling and slightly annoying to others. Like Bruce, I *learned* to generate feelings of well-being. Learning the tools in this book and shifting my focus to what I appreciate about any given moment have helped me develop a more rewarding, healthy, and effective outlook.

There are many reasons to become skilled at creating feelings of appreciation, altruistic behavior, and reflective reactions to frustration. The outcomes of your responses to frustration accumulate over your lifetime. Your reactions have an enormous impact on your mood, and the viability of your relationships. They not only affect your success at work, but also the quality of personal life, and whether or not individuals are available to support you during a personal or professional crisis. In combination, these factors can be a significant asset, or a serious impediment, to your career.

Chapter Four

Unspoken Reasons,
Hidden Realities:
Stories That Stick

We dance around in a ring and suppose
But the secret sits in the middle and knows.

—Robert Frost

N ot all behavior is innocent. Addicts of all kinds, con artists, and individuals with mental illness and character disorders are very real. Sometimes people *are* cooking the books.

Organizations wisely create policies and procedures, including performance management systems, drug testing, written reviews, audits, exit interviews, 360 feedback, EEO policies, expense reports, and written warnings to set standards and hold people to them. If policies or laws *are* being violated, organizations need to act.

The media is full of stories involving fraud and deception. However, the attention these dramatic accounts receive in the media often prevents us from seeing that often our worst fears are *not* realized.

Let's look at the numbers. I've resolved more than 120 very complex conflicts—some involving hundreds of people. Only twice was the situation not related to misunderstandings and hidden realities. In both of those cases the tension was the result of serious performance and ethical issues.

(In situations where one person is behaving in ways that harm others, and the individual can't change, or chooses not to, I report my findings to my client and withdraw as a consultant. I recommend that the organization either goes forward with a coach who is also a clinical psychologist, or that the client uses his or her performance management process to begin leveling consequences for the offending behavior.)

In the other 118 situations there *was* a "baby in the backseat," not malice, wholesale incompetence, or deceit. Therefore, I always enter conflict situations with the assumption that I'm dealing with negative reciprocity, rumors, system problems, and misperceptions. Until proven otherwise I give people the benefit of the doubt, and it's seldom that they didn't deserve it.

> *Clarify, don't vilify.*
>
> —Nancy Clemens

I've learned to behave this way from experience. However, most individuals don't have the advantage of seeing scores of conflicts through to resolution. Consequently, when a colleague or supervisor witnesses an individual behaving in ways that seem irrational, most observers slip into blame-based problem-solving and searching for stupidity.

Almost always, the next step is subtle avoidance, followed by the modern attack behaviors. These two steps doom the chances of resolution. Like Ted and Rhonda from Chapter Two, if I'm avoiding the other person and undermining his or her reputation, the possibility of dialogue and problem resolution is nil. I never learn about the hidden constraints or pressures behind the other party's behavior. Either one of us leaves the organization, or we declare a permanent stony "truce."

The following stories illustrate the distorted realities that occur as people withdraw and speculate about the motives and the reasons behind other people's reactions. Perceptions based on speculation and assumptions are worse than useless. They become part of the problem by drawing others in to validate the conclusion, and by feeding indignation and fear. People continue down their cloak-and-dagger path and their thinking becomes increasingly distorted as time passes.

This void of information is truly a tragedy, because as these stories show, once an individual learns the other party's hidden reasons, contempt usually transforms into compassion and a desire to help.

The exasperated RN

A psychiatric nurse who attended one of my seminars came up to me on break and said, "Anna, I can't overstate the truth of your message. What you're saying reminds me of something I frequently experience at work. After I've had a few days off and return to the unit, I look at the new patients standing in the halls, or slouched in the lounge and think, 'Look at these people! They are pathetic! Can't they shape up and at least take some pride in their appearance?'

"Then I go into the office for report. During this meeting nurses who are ending their shift update those of us who are coming on. By the time the previous shift has finished telling us the background of the new patients, I am humbled by the amount of trauma many of the patients have endured, and embarrassed by my previous judgments.

"I go back on the ward and my disgust has turned into respect and awe. I am amazed that many of the patients are functioning at all, and I'm impressed by their tenacity and will."

I have often thought about this nurse's words. They are a dramatic testimony to the fact that contempt is often the result of ignorance. I've witnessed this many times when I've brought feuding parties to the table and watched as they've heard each other's hidden realities for the first time.

The shut-out employee

Several years ago I helped resolve a conflict between a supervisor, Joni, and her direct report, Ben. For several years they had enjoyed a close working relationship, even attending each other's family weddings and graduations. However, during the six months prior to my arrival, they had withdrawn from each other. Both of them had invested considerable energy in complaining to human resources and to Joni's boss about the other person's lack of cooperation. The HR director told me that Ben and Joni were both feeling anxious, depressed, and victimized by each other.

In my interview with Ben, a fidgety, high-energy employee, he explained that their relationship began to deteriorate shortly after their agency moved into a new office building. At the time, Ben had taken several personal days off to attend a family reunion. Unfortunately, his leave fell during the agency's busiest weeks. Ben feared that Joni, who worked overtime to make up for Ben's time off, held his absence, and his commitment to family, against him. He knew that if this was correct, Joni was discriminating against him, but he feared he didn't have adequate evidence to prove his case.

In our interview, Ben told me that shortly after the move to the new facility, Joni began working in her office with the door closed. Prior to the move they had shared an open work space. Ben interpreted her new isolation as proof that she was becoming inaccessible and remote. I knew there were many possible reasons for her behavior and asked Ben to inquire about her new habit at our next three-way meeting.

At our next meeting Ben told Joni his interpretation that she had become unfriendly and had withdrawn. He cited her closed door as "proof" of her unreasonable behavior. It was an astonishing moment. A look of disbelief crossed Joni's face, and then she burst out laughing! Joni realized how ludicrous and distorted their standoff had become. She jumped up to show us what had actually happened.

Joni explained that when she moved into her new office, the door hung off plumb. When she arrived at work she would open it and push it against the wall, but within a few minutes it would slowly swing half shut. She put in a maintenance report to have it fixed, but she knew it would be added to the bottom of a long list of move-related requests.

One morning, Joni opened her door; walked to her desk, picked up the papers she needed for her meeting, turned and POW! Joni walked smack into the edge of her partially closed door. Rubbing her sore forehead, she decided to keep her door closed until maintenance could repair it.

Unfortunately, this seemingly minor sequence of events happened at the same time Ben had become concerned about their working relationship. He interpreted the closed door as proof that his supervisor was brooding and his career was unjustly doomed.

Ben also made two common mistakes in his interactions with Joni and his coworkers. First, he began to avoid contact with her. His withdrawal limited his opportunities to find out the innocent reason behind her behavior. Second, he started recruiting support from his coworkers and peers that Joni was an unreasonable, distant, and biased supervisor.

Joni noticed Ben's sudden coolness, and when several of Ben's co-workers told her about Ben's campaign to discredit her reputation, she felt betrayed. As a result she became increasingly more guarded in her interactions with Ben. As her warmth toward Ben cooled, he panicked. During the subsequent weeks each of them continued to blame and obsess about the other person, and recruit allies to support their views.

Joni, Ben, and I participated in a series of brief meetings where they listened and reacted to each other's history of inaccurate perceptions. Months of interpretations, assumptions, and speculations were aired, and the reasons behind their behaviors became clear. By the end of our third meeting it was clear that they could have avoided weeks of unnecessary drama and anxiety if they had had the courage and skills to talk to each other directly.

This type of standoff, based on withdrawal—and its twin—erroneous speculation—is not unusual. When tensions increase, the most commonly cited reason individuals do not reach out to each other is the fear that *any contact will make the situation worse.*

In Chapter Nine you'll learn to address sensitive issues in a way that is both safe and powerful. Never again will you have to worry what a person's behavior means. Rather than resorting to uninformed and inaccurate speculations, you will know how to ask the other party for help in understanding his or her behavior.

The traveler who reeked

If we respond to frustration with anger and self-righteousness, not only will we frequently misinterpret behavior, we won't consider that *we* might be part of the problem. We'll assume that we feel frustrated because we're stuck in a chaotic, insane world full of aliens and idiots, and seldom link our irritable mood to our own behaviors. We will overlook possible causes of a situation, and thus overlook potential solutions.

Recently, a participant in a seminar told me a hilarious story that clearly makes this point. Her best friend's husband, Roger, hates to fly, and on a recent business trip his dread was exacerbated when he learned that all the aisle seats were taken. He reluctantly flopped himself in the middle seat. Minutes later, he groaned silently when his in-flight neighbor turned out to be a very large person, who couldn't help but take up some of Roger's precious space. Resigned to a miserable flight, Roger buried himself in a book.

Not long after takeoff, Roger began getting whiffs of a terrible odor. This was too much—his neighbor STUNK! Roger finished the flight in a foul mood and stormed through the terminal flooded with self-pity and indignation. Stomping toward a cab, he thrust his hands into the pocket of his coat.

"Hmmm, what is this?" he wondered. To his embarrassment and chagrin he pulled out the plastic bag (and its contents) that he had used that morning when he had walked his dog in the neighborhood park!

Arm candy

Many times negative speculation is humbling and embarrassing when the *real* reason for someone's odd behavior is revealed. A client told me the following story:

"I was attending an awards banquet when I noticed a man come into the hall with a very beautiful woman.

"Throughout the evening the couple stayed locked together and several people at my table commented on how they were 'attached at the hip.' Their close physical proximity seemed to take a ludicrous turn when he went up to the podium to receive an award and his stunning companion accompanied him!

"Several of us rolled our eyes and nudged each other. However, a few seconds later, our ridicule turned into mortification when the recipient passed our table and we realized he was blind."

The missing supervisor

Sometimes the actual reason for puzzling behavior turns out to be the opposite of what people assume.

I was working with an executive team at a high-tech manufacturing site, when David, the VP of engineering, sought me out. He was at his wit's end over a lead supervisor's erratic behavior. Eddy had been a star performer for many years, but lately he was coming to work looking haggard and unkempt. In addition, David was hearing complaints that Eddy had lengthy, unexplained absences from the floor.

Rumors were circulating that Eddy was using and dealing drugs, and David began to fear the worst. David told me he had pleaded with Eddy, yelled at him, scolded him, and threatened to fire him. Nothing had made a difference. Eddy remained tight-lipped, and his enigmatic behavior continued without a satisfying explanation.

David was desperate to find a way to resolve the situation, and asked if I'd talk to the tight-lipped supervisor. I told David that I might not be any more successful than he had been in learning the causes of Eddy's behavior, but I was certainly willing to meet with him.

At first, Eddy was evasive and cocky. Eventually he began to relax and he became more straightforward. I told him many people were concerned about his uncharacteristic behavior and they were speculating about the cause. I told him about David's concern and asked if there was some way we could alleviate his apprehension. I shared my concern that without a quick turnaround, David would be forced to take a disciplinary action against Eddy, even though David dreaded the thought that he would have to reprimand one of his most senior star performers.

Eventually, Eddy revealed his hidden reality. "I'm being treated for Hepatitis B," he admitted, "which I contracted from a blood transfusion last year. I haven't told anyone because most people get Hepatitis B from dirty needles while taking illegal drugs." I sat quietly waiting for Eddy to go on.

"The doctor told me the medication, which lasts for months, would make me violently ill. He advised me to take sick leave, but because I'm the shift lead, and we're short on staff, I want to be here. I can handle it most days, but sometimes I'm so nauseous I have to find a remote place to sit down."

Eddy and I sat in silence for a few minutes. What had seemed like callous disregard for his crew and manager was really tenacious devotion. We found a way to protect his privacy *and* let David know that his absences from the floor had a legitimate cause, which would soon be coming to an end. When I met with David and shared the information Eddy had given me permission to release, David was close to tears. I realized that these two tough and burly men were actually deeply bonded and had tremendous respect and affection for each other.

Despite the fact that their public behavior was often crude, even antagonistic, when the chips were down, their commitment to each other was unmistakable. I could see their mutual appreciation for each other in David's profound relief that his employee would soon be back to normal and in Eddy's unwillingness to leave his boss short-handed.

This level of commitment to work and people is not uncommon. Over and over I've found that defensive or aggressive people aren't necessarily acting out of malice when they misbehave. They have been hurt. They have concluded that their opinions, commitment, or trust has been unappreciated or misused, and the resulting pain is expressed as cynicism and bitterness.

The following is another story of loyalty, misconstrued as selfcenteredness.

The defiant power plant operators

Sharon, a warm and highly competent human resource director, asked me to resolve a simmering and costly conflict between the managers and workers of a large coal burning power plant. During private interviews with executive team members they told me that relationships between management and crew were at an all-time low.

As evidence, they cited long and protracted contract negotiations; the fact that shortly after negotiations concluded the CFO's car was vandalized in the parking lot; the lack of plant attendance at their monthly all-staff meetings; and most recently, the discovery that a large generator had been found running, drained of oil. If the generator had seized and overheated in their old plant, which was filled with coal dust and ancient wooden beams, the results could have been catastrophic. The last discovery had chilled management to the bone.

The executive team was mystified and offended by the disloyalty shown by the plant operators and responded by withdrawing. They felt the operators were hiding the perpetrator of the drained generator, and in retaliation for their hostility, the top administrators began canceling the social events where the shop and office staff had traditionally mingled.

I set up a series of one-on-one, confidential interviews with a cross-section of plant operators, and their hidden reality began to emerge. The operators agreed that the contract negotiations had dragged on painfully. However, in contrast to the assumptions of the executive team, almost all of the operators expressed satisfaction with the final results. The crew was concerned when they heard about the keying of the CFO's car, but they were insulted that management assumed it had been an act of operator retaliation because his car was parked in a public lot.

However, the biggest contrast to manager's assumptions was their reactions to the drained generator. The operators told me privately that they weren't *hiding* the perpetrator, they were *afraid* of him. Although several of the men had suspicions about who had drained the generator, they had no proof, and they were disappointed that management hadn't done more to identify the perpetrator.

More than one operator pointed out a glaring inconsistency in the management team's speculations: if the generator had overheated and started to burn, the people most at risk would be the operators, not the office staff.

When I met with the CEO and CFO to give them a summary of the interviews, they were incredulous, slightly embarrassed, and similar to David and Eddy from the previous example, flooded with relief.

I set up a series of face-to-face meetings between members of the executive team and the plant supervisors, which became frank, and often startling, discussions. During the next few meetings we resolved many long-standing issues that had driven wedges between the two groups. The CEO assured the plant workers that their safety was critically important, apologized for underreacting to the drained generator, initiated a formal investigation, and took steps to provide more security.

As I wrapped up my work, I was aware that the energy of indignation had blocked curiosity, sparked inaccurate speculation, and short-circuited the natural desire for connection and understanding.

These stories are moving, but not uncommon. We'll cover a few simple skills in Chapter Nine that will allow you to reach out and find what's on the other side of withdrawal, anger, or hostility. With respect and humility you will earn the privilege of glimpsing other people's realities that are currently out of view.

The scowling father of the bride

A client e-mailed me the following story after attending one of my seminars:

"I work as a professional photographer and I agreed to photograph weddings only reluctantly, because they are the most difficult and complex assignments I receive.

"On the wedding day, despite our hard work and planning, one shot after another was being ruined by the scowling father of the bride. My anger was increasing with every frame, and I started resenting his obvious disapproval. I kept thinking, 'What *is* his problem? Maybe he opposes the wedding or dislikes his new son-in-law, but can't he slap on a happy face for his daughter's *wedding*? He can complain about her poor choice of husbands later.'

"I almost said something to the father, but fortunately I held my tongue. A few weeks later I found out from a mutual acquaintance that the bride's father had died from cancer. It turned out that his illness had been causing him a great deal of pain—hence, the frowns. The father had begged his doctor to discharge him from the hospital long enough to walk his beautiful, grieving daughter down the aisle, but he had been unable to completely mask his pain.

"When I heard the rest of the story I was touched by the devotion and love of the family, and learned an important lesson about the futility of judging others."

Although there are many additional stories from my work, I'll close with the following. It's another story of devotion, which was misinterpreted by the uninformed.

The brooding CEO

Butch arrived late at a public seminar and spent the first hour and a half oblivious to the material. Instead of paying attention he organized dozens of Post-it notes in his calendar. Eventually, he finished his task, picked up his pen, and started participating. However, throughout the morning he only seemed marginally attentive.

On break I approached him and learned that he was the CEO of "Stamp-It," a small machine shop that had previously been run by his father. Butch informed me that he had come to the seminar to learn something about conflict resolution, but he didn't say much more. I would learn later that he was truly a man of few words.

Two weeks after the seminar Butch called me and asked if I'd give him feedback on a memo. I suspected that the memo was the tip of a very large iceberg, but I agreed to respond.

The memo was curt and to the point, of course. In it Butch stated that shop employees had begun washing their hands *before* the bell rang for their 15-minute break. This, according to the memo, was unacceptable and the workers were to refrain immediately.

When Butch reached the end of the memo he asked me what I thought. For a second I was tempted to assume there was something wrong with *Butch.* However, I assumed there must be a reason, a story, behind *his* odd behavior. I postponed giving my opinion of his memo and asked him a series of questions instead.

Butch had been CEO of the facility for six years. He had come to his father's company, "Stamp-It!" at his ailing father's urging, reluctantly leaving behind a lucrative job as CFO of another organization. At first, things had gone well—he started making improvements and his rapport and respect with the men had grown. But during contract negotiations, his 43 shop workers unexpectedly went on strike.

After a three-week standoff, the shop workers settled and returned to work. However, Butch was furious. He started canceling the few simple pleasures that the crew had enjoyed for years. First he eliminated the doughnuts the company bought to celebrate birthdays. The next casualty was the company picnic. The letter he had just read to me was his third crackdown.

Butch was angry because every one of his contractions resulted in a pushback from the men, who matched his pettiness every step of the way. The workers prolonged smoke and bathroom breaks, ignored maintenance on the machines, and knowingly ran incorrect orders.

Without realizing it, Butch was engaged in the classic workplace power struggle where each side squares off, matches, and then "tops" the negative behavior of the other party. Behavior declines rapidly in these types of jostling matches. Reciprocity (the tendency to match another person's behavior for good or naught) is a very reliable human response.

At the end of our conversation I told Butch that, unfortunately, I didn't think his memo would help. I suggested that instead he and I work together to find the root cause of the standoff.

A few days later I arrived at the company plant. It was a run-down, dirty building filled with clutter and marred by neglect. Obviously, I thought, no one pays much attention to working conditions. I'd soon learn my assumption was dead wrong.

Butch took me on a tour. The further back we went into his facility, the more dilapidated the building became. Rather than think his workers were disloyal to him, I got the sense that this was one loyal, tenacious group of people who continued to show up for work despite the unpleasant working conditions.

After the tour, Butch gave me permission to interview six or seven of his crew individually and privately, to hear their side of the story. One by one these proud and steadfast men sat on rickety stools in a barren office and told me why they were so unhappy.

When Butch's father had been president, the shop was like family to them. Over the years they'd found small, but meaningful ways to take the tedium and monotony out of their day. They evolved into a gruff, tightly knit brotherhood. When the founder retired and Butch came on as CEO, they recalled stories and fond memories of the days when Butch had worked at the shop to help pay for his college tuition.

However, since Butch had taken over, economic times hadn't been good. There had been a freeze on salaries and pullbacks on benefits. After five years of stagnation, the men went on strike. When they settled the contract and returned to work they expected Butch, like his father before him, to be standing at the front door, welcoming them back and graciously relegating his hostility to the past. Instead they discovered Butch had become a sullen, withdrawn, bitter man who cast a chill throughout the shop when he walked the floor.

The workers couldn't understand his mood, and resented his behavior. When they had gone on strike 15 years earlier, the president had been happy to see everyone back at work. The men felt they had exercised a legal right, played by the rules and returned ready to make a go of it. Butch's behavior seemed both irrational and unreasonable.

It wasn't until I went back to Butch with my summary of their perceptions that Butch revealed the rest of *his* story to me. For the first time his behavior made sense.

I was humbled and touched by the hidden reality behind this proud man. I finally knew what "baby" he had hidden in the back seat. However, the rest of the crew needed to hear his rationale if we were going to restore trust and reestablish communications. When I shared my reactions with Butch, he agreed. The two of us hatched a plan.

The following week, Butch closed the plant at noon. Everyone met at the private dining room of a popular, neighborhood restaurant that had been a place of celebration in more affluent times. We shared a well-prepared, but uncomfortably quiet meal, and when we were finished I asked the guys to help me rearrange the furniture.

We put a table in the middle of the private dining room, and the crew pulled their chairs in a circle around the table. Butch and his accountant sat on one side of the table, and Steve (the union representative) and Lou (an operator from the shop floor), sat on the other.

After setting ground rules I asked Steve and Lou to start. I asked them to tell Butch what they had told me about their resentment of Butch's recent behavior.

Then it was Butch's turn. For the first time, all 43 shop workers saw a side of this private man that had previously remained hidden.

Butch talked about his early days at the shop, the camaraderie and friendly teasing he had enjoyed there as a kid, and how the experience had shaped his character and interests. For the first time he revealed the reluctance he had felt about returning as CEO, and how it had been overridden by loyalty to his father who had no retirement income if the plant went out of business.

Butch revealed that the first thing he learned as CEO was that the economic repercussions from the first strike had been the reason his father had never upgraded the facility. His father had owned a prime piece of property where he had quietly planned to rebuild. However, after the first strike he was able to remain solvent only by selling the land to pay the bills. When Butch became CEO his first goal was to acquire enough equity to rebuild the crumbling facility.

When Butch took over he also learned that the company was dangerously close to bankruptcy. Over the next six years he pulled every trick he knew from his CFO hat to turn the company around. He succeeded brilliantly and was preparing a mortgage application when the union president told him the men had voted to strike. Butch's dream, and six years of hard work, was destroyed.

Butch knew the loan officer would ask two questions, "Do you have a union?" and "Have they ever been on strike?" Butch knew that if he answered yes to the second question, his chances of getting a loan would evaporate. Without a modern facility, Butch knew the company would continue to struggle financially.

When he received the call from the union president, Bruce felt betrayed and angry that the crew hadn't done what they had done in other years—refuse the contract but continue to work.

As Butch explained the reasons for his frustration and disappointment the men became totally still. Slowly, the crew's anger and resentment dissipated. What had previously seemed like Butch's selfishness and brooding callousness was bulldogged devotion.

Steve, the union representative, respectfully explained to Butch why they had made *their* decision. The operators had met on a Friday night to vote on the contract. The union president gave them two choices: either accept the contract or go on strike. It was Steve's first year as union rep and he was too green to realize they had a third option: they could return to work without a signed contract and continue to negotiate. He took the union president at his word and encouraged the members to strike. The employees had no idea what was at stake and how their decision would affect the viability of the company.

Sitting in the restaurant that day was the first time each side heard the other's reasoning. Everyone slouched in his or her chairs. The "enemy" evaporated. What remained was misconstrued loyalty, misunderstanding, and the tremendous sense of loss that comes when one realizes that self-righteousness was unwarranted and self-defeating.

We took a break while everyone regrouped intellectually and emotionally. When they came back we spent two hours brainstorming how Butch and the operators could address the chronic issues that needed to be resolved in order to optimize their chances of success. For the first time in months they were working together as a team.

I stayed in touch with Butch during the next few months and then checked in every year or so just to see how things were going. Together, his company created process improvement groups, and management/crew relationships became the best they had been in years. His voice reflected the joy of people working together in alignment, despite tremendous odds.

Later Butch sent me a letter which stated, "Thank you. You saved the relationships and probably the company."

Assumptions

As these stories show, often the other person's hidden reality is humbling. Each time you face one of your 750,000 frustrations, you can make one of three assumptions. First, you can assume that your frustration is caused by someone else's stupidity. This will likely make you feel angry and irrational as you search for the source of the stupidity, and then attack the other party's reputation or standing.

Secondly, you might assume that your own stupidity is causing the problem. This is likely to make you depressed and lethargic.

Finally, you might assume there's a reality hidden from your view: and, if you knew it the other person's behavior would make sense. If you make the third assumption, you will become curious, and perhaps concerned. Only then will you be inclined to reach out and begin a conversation—perhaps the *very* conversation necessary to save your company or team.

Chapter Five

Intelligent Fools:
The Hidden Price Tags of
Irritability and Contempt

If I'm not part of the problem, there is no solution.
—Bathroom graffiti

If blaming others is such a destructive practice, why is it so prevalent? People mistakenly believe that blame and self-righteous indignation will move them closer to their goals, regardless if those goals are status, profitability, esteem, promotions, respect, achievement, or success. *Blaming others is a widespread problem because the perceived payoffs are immediate and visible, and the costs are delayed and hidden.*

Even though my work immerses me in the world of blame and its hidden consequences, it took me many years before I saw all the costs of ridiculing and demeaning others. Once you take an objective look at these hidden price tags of blaming others, it's likely you'll never again be tempted to use it.

Sometimes I am quietly amused when the true source of a problem is made visible. It is then clear that individuals have wasted so much pompous energy, goodwill, time, and resources! They've staked their reputations to publicly dethroning their enemies. However, after their scapegoat is exonerated and both sides of the story are known, they begin a painful—and at the same time, exhilarating—journey of restoring credibility and rebuilding relationships.

My clients almost always have the talent and expertise to fix the problem *without* my intervention, but the obvious becomes invisible when the focus is on personalities, not processes.

Cost #1: Mind-boggling amounts of money are wasted

Organizations profit from extensive improvements when leaders, executives, or department heads reconcile. Behaviors such as off-task activity, mean-spirited retaliation, speculation, gossip, and undermining, are replaced by cooperation, creativity, cross-functional decision-making, and synergy—the primary reasons groups and organizations are created!

However, other costs mount even more dramatically. Many of my clients carefully cover up their embarrassment as they painlessly solve entrenched system problems that have been festering in the background for months or years after we've shifted from personality to situational problem-solving.

The real problems, which are typically systemic, have been draining millions of hard-earned dollars while leaders and employees have had their attention absorbed by escalating rounds of personality-based, destructive behaviors. When the focus is on personality and character, problems are hidden and excused, downplayed or, conversely, exaggerated and distorted. Behaviors such as objective fact-finding, admitting an oversight, sacrificing, lending a hand, and side-by-side problem-solving have all but disappeared.

It's *impossible* to address the real causes of tension and waste when the key players are involved in a high-stakes power struggle. In Chapter Eight we'll look at the cost savings in detail by closely examining two case studies.

Cost #2: Credibility suffers

Sometimes people blame others as a means of avoiding self-assessment, or to sidestep responsibility in playing a less than stellar role in a workplace difficulty. Individuals often hope that by building a slightly distorted case against another person their own behavior won't be scrutinized.

The "Quick! Look-over-there!" scapegoat strategy harms, rather than helps, your reputation and career. I've seen this dozens of times. Colleagues, supervisors, and direct reports learn to doubt your word and suspect, fairly or not, that your version of truth is *often* incomplete or distorted.

Here's what happens out of sight. If you attempt to convince your supervisor, Larry, that the cause of a joint problem lies entirely within someone else's domain, and that you are merely an innocent by-stander, it won't be long before he gathers enough information to discover that you are covering up your role in the problem.

However, it's unlikely that Larry will mention his findings to you. He will anticipate more denials, and he won't waste his time. Consequently, you won't discover how his opinion of you plummeted when he uncovered facts you withheld. Larry will surmise that he can't take you at your word, and will resent having to fact-find on his own, rather than trust you to relay the complete story.

It's likely Larry will share his disappointment with his boss or peers, which will affect your reputation and career in unseen ways. Unfortunately, from your perspective—with no one confronting you directly— you'll believe you were successful in avoiding your share of responsibility for the snafu.

Cost #3: Direct reports and colleagues silently resent blame

No matter how incompetent, unethical, or self-defeating one's own behavior might be, finding a scapegoat gives some people the illusion that they are superior to the object of their contempt. However, it's distressing to watch someone attempt this transparent ploy. The speaker is assuming others don't see through their feeble attempts to denigrate others for their own gain.

Even though your colleagues, boss, and direct reports might display weary smiles as you blame others, your efforts to look superior by making someone else look stupid will wear thin over time. It's similar to a late-stage alcoholic who tries to convince others that *she* doesn't have a drinking problem compared to the homeless, inebriated person sleeping on the street. Although no one in her party confronts her, what they say in her absence is harsh and blunt.

Contempt and derision
Fuel resentment and suspicion.

—Nancy Clemens

Criticizing others in their absence sends a clear, damaging message about *you*. The people who listen to your criticisms become disillusioned because finger pointing solves *nothing* and, therefore, makes their jobs more difficult.

Direct reports and colleagues carry deep, carefully hidden resentments when their supervisor attempts to discredit others as a means of winning allies. Your colleagues and direct reports won't speak up for one very poignant reason—they don't want to become your next target. However, coworkers and direct reports are paying the price for your ineffectiveness and your unwillingness to admit responsibility.

I saw this happen at a high-tech research and design company. Rob, the director of operations, ridiculed the chief engineer with the regularity of an atomic clock. In front of Rob, the operators would grin and shrug as he spun the latest story of the engineer's incompetence. However, in private interview, *every one* of the seven operators said, in essence, "I wish Rob would stop. It's like he *wants* the engineer to fail. Rob is making relationships between our departments more tense and *more* difficult—not easier."

When a boss or colleague makes a habit of targeting others, few people have enough audacity to address the situation directly. However, as the following story reveals, resentment is simmering just below the surface.

The troubled dialysis unit

I was asked to help a dialysis department at a prominent, metropolitan hospital. Alice, the division's vice president, called me into her office and said, "I've tried everything to stop the three leaders of the unit from fighting, and you're my last hope. If you can't resolve the conflict between the head nurse, the assistant head nurse, and the technical supervisor, I am going to close the unit and tell the doctors to take their patients elsewhere. The closing would cost us millions in lost revenues, but I can't allow the unit to continue. The staff is so preoccupied with this conflict that patient safety is at risk."

I assured Alice that I would do my best. After gathering background information, I met with each of the three supervisors alone to get their candid perspectives. During the private interviews, each of them said to me, "I know *I* have the majority of the staff behind me. " When I inquired why they were so sure of their conclusion all three of them said, "They *tell* me they prefer working with me over the other two leaders."

I wasn't a math major, but I knew the three leaders were being "played." My first step was to break through the illusion they each held, that they had a majority of the staff's support behind them.

With their knowledge and input, I drew up a confidential survey for their 65 direct reports. When the surveys were returned to my office, the staff's anger and resentment toward *all three* supervisors was stunning. Assured of confidentiality, the nurses and technicians revealed they were furious that the three leaders had each worked to pit the shifts, nurses, and technicians against the other managers. The staff comments were laced with bitter complaints about the immaturity and irresponsibility of the three leaders. Most of the employees were particularly enraged that the leaders had compromised patient safety in order to play out a private vendetta against one another.

I typed up their comments (removing any identifying information), made copies, and asked the three supervisors to meet with me as a group. After a few words of warning, I handed each of them a copy of the staff's comments. As they read through the responses, their self-righteousness and smugness evaporated. All three shifted uncomfortably in their seats.

After a few minutes I shared my perspective. They had been in a power struggle to save their careers at the expense of their peers. In reality, even if they had succeeded in getting the other supervisors fired, they would not have been able to salvage their own reputations. Even if they were successful in driving out one or two of the other managers, the targeted person wouldn't retreat meekly. The exiled supervisor would stay in touch with his or her former faction members and continue to defend their reputations from a distance. Their loyal coalition members would continue to undermine the surviving leader and create a smoldering, intractable mutiny. The situations are hard to detect and almost impossible to eradicate.

I shared my belief that the only way the three leaders could salvage their reputations was to combine their talents and skills to restore the productivity, morale, and efficiency of their *unit*. If they wanted to regain the respect of the vice president, their direct reports and peers, they had to lay aside their animosity and turn their department into a world-class team.

Our two-hour meeting was a major turning point. Confronted with irrefutable evidence that the gig was up, and, in fact had *never* worked, they looked exhausted and self-conscious. The next morning there was a noticeable shift in the energy and mood. Their smugness and defensiveness were replaced with a sense of resignation and chagrin. We began working to identify the specific incidents and the role confusion that had driven them apart. Then we created a plan to heal the damage that their contempt had caused their direct reports.

Cost #4: Blame turns potential allies into enemies

Individuals who rely on blame as a means to solve problems believe that by undermining others, they will remove the risk of scrutiny from their plates. However, it's foolish to assume that the derogatory comments you make about your target don't leak back! Ridicule is not only passed along, it is embellished and amplified. Negative comments about others alienate people who are, or could have become, significant sources of information and support. Zingers about others, even witty ones, create permanent breaches of trust.

The following scenario is more common than not. Imagine you make a negative, but seemingly harmless comment to a colleague, Barry, about Sheila the shipping manager. Barry loves to "stir the pot" and passes the juicy bit on to Megan. Megan carpools with Sheila and can hardly wait to tell her about your comment on the way home.

Sheila will reciprocate your denigrating remark by making her own negative comments about you and attacking *your* character or competence. Megan will be caught in the middle of a volley and will be very tempted to use the spicy gossip to gain attention, or enhance her status with her peers. Soon there will be an invisible wall of hurt and mistrust, not only between you and Sheila, but the people who are loyal to each of you. Your closest friends and colleagues will bring you every rumor or negative innuendo to prevent you from being blindsided. As your behavior changes in response to an ongoing stream of negative speculation, you will look paranoid and irrational.

As the following story reveals, you may never know the true damage to your reputation, relationships, and effectiveness.

The president's torn loyalties

I was asked by a company president to help his family-owned, high-tech printing company. The VP of sales was the president's son, Mark, a handsome, polished young man, and proud possessor of a newly acquired M.B.A. The president's business partner of 30 years, Bob, was COO. Bob was an easygoing, reliable, salt-of-the-earth graduate from the school of hard knocks. These two leaders couldn't have been more different in upbringing and outlook. When I arrived at their company, their disagreements about the future direction of the organization had grown into a two year power struggle. As in many escalated conflicts, Mark and Bob were each privately lobbying the president to terminate the other.

At the height of the conflict, Mark had reluctantly invited Bob to a sales meeting with one of their biggest customers. Because Bob had years of experiences with ink, printers, and paper and Mark was relatively new to the trade, Mark needed Bob's input to make the sale. However, Mark's desire to see his nemesis fail couldn't help but impact their project. Mark didn't coach Bob on the formality of a high-status meeting. Bob, who had never been included in a high-stakes, polished sales call, arrived in his scruffy attire that was appropriate for the shop floor, but not a corporate environment.

Bob's embarrassment and discomfort over his obvious faux paus increased as the meeting progressed. Bob was in over his head and didn't know how to regain his equilibrium. Unfortunately, he fell back on a technique that worked well back at the plant: he swore! In this setting, however, his outburst hung awkwardly in the air. The meeting came to an premature end. No more than five minutes after returning to the office, Mark approached his father with the latest proof that Bob was too unsophisticated and crude to make a transition to working with corporate clients.

However, Bob wasn't powerless. He skillfully undermined Mark's support and popularity. With his crew—the majority of the employees—Bob painted Mark out to be a hopeless, silver spoon yuppie totally out of touch with the realities of their trade and privileged only because of his father's authority. Consequently, when Mark walked the shop floor, people would barely acknowledge his presence, let alone give him the information he needed to learn the nuances of the trade.

The situation was typical of power struggles. Although the conflict centered on these two men, every employee in the organization knew about this conflict, fed it, gossiped about it, and picked sides.

Every employee in their respective departments carried half-baked prejudices and unjust criticisms of the other person (and eventually the entire department) throughout the organization. Customers were pulled into the web. The two men became invested in the other's decline and began contributing to each other's blunders. It undoubtedly cost the organization thousands, if not millions, of unmeasured dollars in the form of off-task behavior, lost opportunities, and the resulting impact of an invisible, but deep, trench between operations and sales.

The hapless father/owner responded to the tension and torn loyalties in a manner similar to many conflicted leaders—he increased his trips to the golf course! The organization's growth was paralyzed and system problems grew.

I worked with Mark and Bob intermittently over several months. As they began to learn more about each other and address the conflict and rumors between them, they realized the vast majority of their dislike and fear of one another was based on misunderstandings and speculations that had been distorted and amplified as they circulated throughout the organization.

They began to talk in depth about their expertise and vision of the future. Their commitment to the company was obvious even though it was expressed in very different ways. Bob showed his devotion to the company and lifelong business partner through his rock-solid reliability and depth. Mark's commitment to his father's enterprise was expressed through flamboyant, gutsy, and charismatic risk-taking. As I worked with Mark and Bob, their annoyance developed into admiration. Their former hostility over the dramatic differences in their personalities morphed into fascination for the unique combination of Bob's superb craftsmanship and Mark's creativity, chutzpah, and business savvy.

As their bond solidified, we knew they each had to break the habit of bringing forward distorted half-truths and speculations about the other person. I suggested that they not only state frankly that they had begun to strengthen and repair their partnership, but also begin speaking highly of each other in front of their direct reports, peers, and the president.

I enjoyed several lunches with the executive team over the next two years and watched Bob and Mark become each other's strongest defenders. On multiple occasions I observed one or the other spontaneously and genuinely come to the other's defense in their absence. After my formal work wrapped up, I stayed in touch, and learned that they had entered new markets and created products that re-energized their organization. When I did my final follow up three years later they were still going strong.

At the closure of my work, the president struggled to express his profound relief that the long simmering friction between two important people in his life had finally come to an end. I suspect that the resolution of Bob and Mark's conflict not only contributed to the prosperity of the company, it added many years to the president's life.

The details and idiosyncrasies of Bob and Mark's struggle are unique. But the course of their conflict is not. Speculation, fueled by onlookers, fills the vacuum when two interdependent colleagues withdraw. Consequently, sometimes when I dig for true barriers to a working alliance all I find are remnants and wisps of rumors and assumption. I can't help but wonder how many brilliant partnerships crumble under the surprising weight of avoidance.

Cost #5: Blame becomes an automatic response

Individuals often believe that blame is harmless and they use it reflexively as a source of entertainment, particularly in work areas that have little stimulation, variety, or access to information. Blame is often the fallback position for people with low skills or low self-confidence who compensate for their deficiencies and insecurities by ridiculing and tearing others down. Unskilled workers or individuals with low self-confidence often develop a cutting sense of humor (with a keen ability to deflate the intentions of any person or project). Sadly, sarcasm and put-downs become the one thing at which they excel, and they use it habitually to increase their status within the group.

Our minds are remarkably plastic, and cutting humor easily becomes an automatic response. You may regret the relexive, automatic, contempuous wit you use when what you really want to do is assist a collegue, partner, or child, or to speak on their behalf.

Bobby Knight was previously mentioned as an example of an individual who was unable to stop his destructive, aggressive reactions when he was frustrated, even when facing the loss of his job. Minnesota's former governor, Jesse Ventura, is another public figure who discovered that flooding and blame-based reactions to frustration (learned during his wrestling career) were the undoing of his political career. Early in his campaign many people admired his unique, irreverent style and his willingness to challenge the status quo. However, as his term progressed, his aggressive reactions toward anyone who challenged him alienated the press, legislators, and supporters. His inability to stop flooding eventually cost him the broad base he had once enjoyed.

If you reinforce and reiterate reflexive reactions, they become automatic. Over time you will respond reflexively even when it's not your intention to alienate the other party. As a result, you risk becoming more isolated, less effective, and more cynical as others distance themselves from you and your disheartening comments.

Cost #6: Blame demoralizes employees and destroys pride in work

Even though individuals use blame to avoid responsibility or juice up an otherwise lackluster day, the *primary* reason formal and informal leaders use blame is to create a sense of camaraderie with their direct reports. However, your department will become *more* demoralized, not less, if they are told repeatedly that incompetent dimwits and control-freaks run the organization for which they work.

Years ago, I worked for an employee assistance program and my boss, Alexa, and I would frequently bond over our mutual dislike for her supervisor, Michael. Whenever I'd come into her office to complain about him she'd whisper, "Close the door," and pull out memos he had written. We'd laugh and ridicule him. If Alexa and I had approached our problems more professionally, I would have learned the reasons behind the decisions that troubled me the most. However, she and I unknowingly squandered our opportunity to build a better department by turning frustrations and concerns into a black hole of hopelessness and futile attacks. Alexa and I formed a perverse bond, and I didn't realize until later how destructive our behavior had been for my career *and* for the rest of our department.

Because I heard and tracked every negative situation that was brought to my attention, I developed a reputation among management of being critical and cynical. When I left to take a new position, I was convinced that the demise of the employee assistance program was imminent. I believed that Michael's poor decisions, which I had heard about daily and worked so hard to improve, would have dire consequences. In reality, after I left the business not only survived, it thrived and expanded. I was truly puzzled, and perhaps a bit disappointed that the pending drama I had envisioned never materialized.

I realized later that I had unwittingly become a "lightning rod of dissent." Disgruntled employees knew they could bring me major and minor grievances and find a willing ear. However, they often neglected to tell me good news or update me when their concerns *were* resolved. My fears were exacerbated by Alexa's willingness to confirm my fears about Michael's incompetence.

Leaders are conduits of information. Explaining the decisions of management is one of their most important roles. When leaders sidestep this responsibility and ridicule those in authority to create a superficial sense of closeness, direct reports feel foolish for investing in their work.

This doesn't mean you need to agree with every decision. Leaders at all levels need to be in ongoing dialogue and share their genuine support *and* disagreement. However, there is a world of difference between face-to-face discussion and ridiculing other decision-makers behind their backs in order to gain popularity and loyalty within a team. While you may feel temporarily inflated, or even heroic, by rallying the troops against a common enemy, in the long run, blame destroys your department's motivation, morale, and pride in work.

Conflict within the ranks

I didn't clearly see the link between blame and the loss of pride in work until I worked with chiefs of police and department supervisors in Wisconsin.

The first time I was asked to do a seminar with police departments I felt slightly paranoid. Before I left home I kept checking to see if I had my driver's license, car tabs, and insurance documents. Despite my nervousness, the officers were warm, funny, and grateful to learn about flooding, heart disease, and hostilty.

I asked the participants to think about conflicts with colleagues, citizens, supervisors, city hall, and politicians—anyone they interfaced with regularly—except perpetrators and drug addicts. To my surprise, in a group of 80 officers there was a strong consensus that the most demoralizing part of their work was *conflict within the ranks.*

Unexpectedly, three officers were paged out of the seminar. A nearby resident had locked himself in his apartment with a collection of guns, threatening to harm himself or anyone else who came within range. My heart went out to the officers as they left. I learned later that they had been successful in convincing the man to surrender.

That evening as I drove home, the incident triggered a stream of thoughts. I wondered what it would be like to have a job in which you literally risked your life, and then reported to a chief who used reflexive, blaming reactions to bond with his direct reports.

This is a perfect scenario to see the damage of blame upon morale. Imagine an officer returning from this dangerous call and experiencing one of his 30 frustrations for the day. He finds a memo on his desk from their mayor, Joy. The memo starts, "I regret to inform you that your department's request for bulletproof vests has been denied...."

In this situation, it would be *appropriate* for the officer who, just minutes ago, risked his life to be flooded with adrenaline, cortisol, and hormones. During the fight-or-flight response, his blood would thicken to prevent blood loss and his pulse and blood pressure would be elevated. Consequently, the officer, who is partially (and appropriately) flooded is primed to overreact to the disappointing news. He marches in to the chief's office and exclaims, "Have you seen this? What an idiot! Does the mayor know *anything* about police work? Has she ever walked a beat? All she cares about getting reelected, like all politicians!"

This is a critical moment for the chief. If he takes the bait, his reflexive response will be similar to, "I saw that memo. I gave Joy the benefit of the doubt but now I'm convinced she's depriving some village of an idiot. If you think that's bad, wait until I tell you what she said at the golf course last week when she was half plowed."

If the officer and chief make this choice, they will take a critical event down the left side of the "Frustration" diagram in Chapter Two (page 41). They will react with blame, inflammatory thinking, and contempt.

Behaviorally, they are primed for attack and withdraw, and they will probably do both.

If they attack the mayor by spreading negative opinions of her, it's unlikely they'll be in a mind-set to problem-solve with her. After they agree she's a hopeless opportunist, there is little hope they'll be successful in securing a different decision.

This scenario happens across organizations in every department and level, thousands of times every day. The supervisor and direct report are bonding through blame, and they are getting an immediate payoff—the surge of energy created by hostility. However, there's a consequence that will occur after the meeting which leaders often miss. Although the supervisor has bonded with his employee, he has failed to bridge him to the broader leadership and mission of the city.

After Mike leaves his supervisor's office he has to go back on his beat. Halfway to his squad car it will hit him: "Wait a minute. I'm putting my life on the line for a jerk! Now *I'm* the chump! Why should I care about this place? Some half-baked, petty politician is our leader! I think I'll call in sick."

With multiple repetitions, the chief will discover that he has a demoralized workforce. His officers will be cynical about the organization, and resent the perception of unethical and incompetent leadership. The chief will discover his officer's pride in their organization is waning, or they are becoming increasingly fixated on the financial aspects of their job. Without knowing it, the chief is inadvertently destroying the intrinsic rewards of work (service, pride, camaraderie, identity, and meaning). The officers will fear the worst is yet to come.

Sadly, most leaders in this position don't see the connection between treating other decision-makers with contempt and a growing loss of morale. Leaders and colleagues who use contempt as a bonding ritual often become *more* derogatory and critical of leadership as their unit deteriorates.

Employees want their sacrifices, overtime, and commitment to matter. When they are told their leader is incompetent or unethical, they feel foolish for caring, and then withdraw.

If you use ridicule to explain shortages or delays, you'll reduce the possibility that your staff will be able to make sense out of their organization and leverage its strengths. Without information about organizational constraints, pressures, and strategies, employees cannot align their efforts in a meaningful way, nor will they feel pride in belonging to a workplace worthy of their deep investments.

Rather than build morale, blame triggers feelings of helplessness and hopelessness. When you attribute the source of a problem to people, it means *they* must change in order for *your* problem to be fixed. Because this is unlikely, employees will conclude that they are stuck with intractable problems, and their desire to improve and invest in their organization will falter.

Cost #7: Colleagues and direct reports no longer trust you

Returning to the previous example of the chief and his officer, imagine that after they've done a thorough job of discrediting the intentions and character of Joy, the mayor, she unexpectedly drops in. The chief quickly shifts gears and responds to his supervisor with warmth and a statement that he is pleasantly surprised to see her.

While the chief is covering up his negative behavior and making nice, the officer is busy "reading" his chief. The officer won't miss a single nuance. He concludes that the chief is a hypocrite, and willing to flatter and charm the same people he was ridiculing just seconds ago.

The officer wonders whether the chief does the same thing behind the his back. The officer never again feels certain that his supervisor speaks well of him in his absence, or will come to his defense.

There's a parable from Ireland that summarizes this well, "People who are talking to you about others, are talking to others about you." Even if the officer previously looked up to the chief, he now seems like a blow-hard without integrity.

Cost #8: Partners-in-crime sell you down the river

The most expensive, and invisible, cost of blame is betrayal—when colleagues or direct reports take privileged ridicule to the targeted person. I have seen this end a promising career without any awareness on the part of the person who was being betrayed.

I was asked to untangle a conflict between two up-and-coming attorneys by Sheila, one of the firm's senior partners. One of the attorneys, Adam, had been at the firm for many years. He was quite withdrawn and his social skills were poor. However, Adam's work was consistent and reliable. Three years before my arrival, his colleague, Lance, had joined the firm after being recruited aggressively by the partners. When Lance came on board he brought a national reputation from which the firm had benefited.

Although Lance and Adam could easily have become competitors, they created an uneasy alliance by nurturing their deep dislike for one of the senior partners, Pamela. Their aversion was so intense that every morning they'd shut themselves in their offices for the daily round of "Pummeling Pamela." Adam and Lance saw this particular form of entertainment as a job perk and enjoyed the cohesiveness it created.

However, during Lance's third year, Adam made a series of errors. At first Lance tried to hide his colleague's mistakes, but eventually he had no choice but to inform their adversary, Pamela.

Adam, who was used to being a respected performer, handled his fall from grace poorly. He withdrew from the social life of the office and became despondent. Increasingly, the most prestigious work was referred to Lance.

Several months into this painful decline, Adam made a desperate attempt to regain some of his former status by tarnishing Lance's rising star. Unfortunately, Lance had given Adam plenty of data to accomplish his goal.

Adam dropped into Pamela's office and asked if he could share something in confidence. Pamela agreed and Adam revealed some of the most noxious comments Lance had made behind her back. To solidify his credibility, he included information that Pamela had told Lance in confidence and that Adam could not have learned elsewhere.

Despite the fact that Adam's self-oriented motives were transparent, he achieved his goal. Because Pamela had agreed to confidentiality before the conversation began, she decided not to confront Lance directly. Instead, she retaliated subtly, and quietly shelved his career.

Lance continued to work at the firm, oblivious to the fact that his now estranged colleague, Adam, had poisoned Lance's relationship with *the* person who had the most influence over his future. Lance had played a significant role in his own downfall by wallowing in negativity on a daily basis with Adam.

Although this is the most extreme act of betrayal I've witnessed, I've seen many that are less dramatic. These situations have taught me that the only way you can keep others from repeating your disparaging comments is to never give them material to exploit. Refusing to initiate or take part in backstabbing not only preserves your reputation for integrity and honesty, but it's essential to maintain a clean and unabashed relationship with your supervisor, or anyone else who affects your career. Once you target another person, your relationship begins to change. You can never be certain if they've heard your disparaging remarks, and that subtle doubt will affect your interactions. You will become slightly more guarded, less warm, and uneasy in their presence.

Here's the ground rule I'd suggest for sideways comments: if you wouldn't be willing to make your comment directly to the person, *don't* say it to someone else. It's too likely that it *will* be relayed to the person of whom you speak—and because you won't be informed, you will be powerless to undo the harm.

In climates of blame, *no one* is exempt

The hidden price tags of blame demonstrate the long-term futility and destructiveness of a personality-based orientation. By looking at examples from history, we can see how these costs escalate to tragic dimensions. Whether it's an office unit or government that disseminates a climate of blame, no one is safe from becoming a target.

In Chapter Two I used Hitler as an example of an infamous architect of blame, and I want to return to him as an example of how targets are replaced when previous scapegoats are eliminated—and yet the problem remains.

Early in Hitler's reign, he targeted small, vulnerable groups such as the developmentally disabled or the mentally retarded, and identified them as the source of the country's economic problems. He annihilated most of this population in Germany, claiming they were a drain on society. When none of the country's economic problems changed, Hitler shifted his focus to Gypsies, an unpopular group with few political allies. Of course, after they were removed from German society none of the country's economic problems improved, because the economic situation Germany faced was the result of *widespread, systemic problems,* not the behavior of a small subgroup.

However, like most people with blame orientations, Hitler didn't learn from his lack of success. Instead, he became more desperate as he failed to deliver on his promised improvements. Hitler shifted the direction of his hostility again. He targeted gay and lesbian people, Catholics, and finally Jewish communities.

Hitler believed he could reach his goals by targeting those who disagreed with him or appeared to stand in his way. Although he was able to carry his distorted plans to fruition, he did not deliver the changes he promised. As a result, he brought an entire country, and much of Europe, to ruin. In an ever-escalating spiral of blame he squandered the opportunity to bring about the systemic changes that *would* have made a difference.

Although Hitler is an extreme example, there are strains of the same reflexive damage in every organization—or government—that tolerates blame as an acceptable response to frustration.

Targets of blame in society

In our society, blame is on the rise. Conservatives blame liberals, liberals blame neo-conservatives, parents blame schools, schools blame society, the rich blame the poor, the poor blame the middle and upper classes. Wives blame husbands, husbands blame the boss, farmers blame immigrants, corporations blame government, and Arabs blame the Jews. We blame based on race, religion, ethnicity, gender, sexual orientation, and age. We blame politicians in general, minorities, the police, attorneys, and so on.

Targets of blame at work

Workplaces can divide into destructive factions based on almost every conceivable difference: occupation, shift, geographic location, longevity, gender, race, level, and job-function. I've even seen groups break into coalitions based on the kind of truck they drove to work or the sports team they supported.

If you look at the reasons individuals assign blame to certain groups, one thing stands out. Any perceivable difference, such as a *physical difference* (gender, ethnic, or racial origins), or any *philosophical difference* (the perspectives of an engineer versus sales, or a psychologist versus a social worker) can be used to justify blame.

If you blame others for problems in your systems, you teach your colleagues, direct reports, and loved ones that when they are frustrated, it is appropriate to respond with blame. It's not difficult to foresee that when *they* are frustrated, they will turn the arrow of contempt in *your* direction. After all, *you've* taught them that this is an appropriate response.

Once blame takes hold of an organization or a society, *no one* is safe. Blame ricochets through groups and pulls in unwilling participants who feel they must monitor the gossip and retaliate in order to defend their reputations and alliances.

If you blame others when you are frustrated, you are setting yourself up for a lifetime of disappointment and mistrust. Blame destroys the positive energy and interactions that are essential to workplace cohesiveness, alignment, and success.

The next chapter will explain a simple, positive alternative to blame. You will see how you can change your reaction from reflexive to reflective, and bond *and* bridge with your direct reports during moments of frustration. You can preserve their pride in the organization, your reputation as a leader of integrity, *and* solve the problem—to the benefit of your career, department, employees, and organization.

Chapter Six

A Touch of Genius and a Lot of Courage: How to Unplug From Resentment, Stress, and Mistrust

One kind word can
Warm three winter months

—Japanese proverb

If you experience feelings of smoldering anger, self-righteous indignation, and contempt, then your effectiveness, health, relationships, and mood—the quality of your *life*—depend on your ability to replace the energy of hostility with the energy of appreciation. This is not an overstatement.

Fortunately, it's not difficult. It can be one of the most rewarding and validating projects you will undertake. I too had to make the transition. When I reflect on the information and insights that preceded my commitment to change, I feel profound gratitude.

You're halfway there if you've read this far. You know about flooding, heart disease, depression, the hidden costs of blame, inflammatory thinking, cynicism, low self-esteem, and "babies in the backseat." You know there are three nearly invisible thinking patterns that determine your mood and behavior.

In this chapter we'll cover specific techniques that will help you replace negative energy with habits that are more rewarding.

First, let's address changes in your personal life that will support a change from unhealthy to healthy patterns. Again, you can't just stop flooding. That strategy leaves you with no energy, and that's the condition we hate the most. To maintain your gain you must replace hostility with hearty appreciation.

First we'll look at how you can replace negative energy with warmth, achievement, and activities that give you energy and sustain you—activities that *aren't* associated with hostility. Then we'll look at the phases most people go through as they rewire their brains to stop flooding.

Switch channels and activities

1. **Eat real food.** If breakfast consists of a doughnut and super-sized Mountain Dew, and dinner is four beers, a greasy hamburger, and a bag of chips, your body doesn't have access to the nutrients it needs to sustain calming energy. Junk food, just like cheap gas, doesn't work for the long haul.

2. **Change channels.** If you tune in to music, radio, or TV programs that use inflammatory thinking to draw an audience, stop listening. In a study by HeartMath, just 15 minutes of listening to grunge rock resulted in increased feelings of hostility, fatigue, sadness, tension, and led to *significant reductions in mental clarity*. Why allow toxic, negative energy into your life? Are you in a better mood, more effective, or more fun to be around after listening to an hour of hate-radio? Inflammatory programs tap reflexive responses. Hate radio isn't interested in your health or well-being, your ability to parent, or your career. Shock-jock radio programs are on a mission to increase ratings and revenues, and they are willing to do it at your expense.

   If you listen to inflammatory radio on your way to work, when you walk in the door you will already be irritated; your hormones, adrenaline, and blood pressure will be elevated; and you'll be less able to handle your day's allotment of frustrations.

   If you tune in to the same station on your way home, you'll add more negative energy to your overtaxed system and when you face the demands of children, partners, and home—boom! You'll flood. Instead, find something during your commute that soothes you and doesn't tap the energy of aggression and increase your agitation. Find another radio station, bring your own CDs, or get audio books from the library. Five minutes before you arrive home, pull over and practice gratitude. It's a very effective way to stop toxic thoughts and elevate your mood.

3. **Exercise!** It's one of *the most effective* antidotes for elevating your mood. (Watching television is one of the least effective, but most frequently used, activities for combating a negative mood). Join sports teams that aren't so much into cutthroat winning, as they look forward to goofing off, having fun, and building friendships. Get a pet, hike, hunt, knit, camp in the woods, start a yard project, garden, tinker in the garage and create something to give away, bike, or take your kids for a walk around a lake and watch the moon rise.

4. **Avoid harsh self-criticism.** Make a commitment to identify and eliminate self-blame, as it leads to depression, lack of energy, and the desire to blame others as a means of escaping feelings of hopelessness. In Chapter Eight we'll look at a technique that helps eliminate negative feelings about yourself.

5. **Take advantage of the helper's high.** You *deserve* the feelings of bliss that are associated with compassion and offering a helping hand. Find volunteer work that fits your schedule, interests, and talents. Go out of your way to befriend someone at work. Remember, even small acts of kindness release endorphins.

   In a study of more than 2,000 Presbyterians published in 2004 in the journal *Psychosomatic Medicine*, behavioral scientist Carolyn Schwartz and her colleagues reported that improved mental health seemed to be more closely linked to giving help than to receiving it.

   Don't stop yourself because you think you have nothing to offer. It takes very little to make a difference in another person's life. Dr. Jennifer Crocker at the University of Michigan, Ann Arbor, in a study of high-risk youth from impoverished neighborhoods and barren families, found that the minority of adolescents who *did not* end up in the juvenile correction system, who resisted crime and drugs, and finished high school, had one consistent environmental trait in common: they answered the following question in the affirmative: "Do you have someone to talk to about the things that trouble you?" One link to a caring human being allowed them to thrive in an environment that overwhelmed their peers.

6. **Surround yourself with positive people who know how to build and maintain positive relationships.** Every human aches for positive companionship, laughter, and vitality. It's what nature intended. Do what it takes to replace sources of negative energy in your life with warmth and affection.

You will find positive people who are worthy of your investment at work, in clubs, in faith communities; in your neighborhood; and volunteering at hospitals, food shelves, and youth programs.

People with strong support systems are more able to avoid disease and maintain higher levels of health. *Social support is a natural antidote to tension and stress.*

Be discerning about the people you associate with in your personal life. Start observing people's energy and language. Watch how different people approach problem-solving. Do they blame *people* or do they look for problems or pressures in the situation? On the road are they patient or hostile? Stay away from those drivers who think anyone who goes slower than they do is an idiot, and anyone who goes faster is a lunatic!

Pay attention to how people approach political problems. Do they label people who are different? Are they curious or indignant? Do they see most people as reasonable, and view desperate behavior as a result of desperate conditions, or are they quick to call other people derogatory names?

Find and associate with people who laugh, invest in others, are effective at solving problems, enjoy long-term intimate relationships, and don't overreact to life's inevitable hassles. These people aren't naive. As Einstein noted in the quote that opens Chapter One, a harmonious, positive life requires skill. Any intelligent fool can move in the other direction.

7. **Start rituals of appreciation.** Say a prayer of thanks before meals; make a mental list of all the things for which you are grateful before you fall asleep; write notes, e-mails, and letters to loved ones. Martin Seligman, one of the founders of Positive Psychology, found that people who wrote and delivered a letter of appreciation to someone who had changed their lives had long-lasting increases in happiness. Expressions of appreciation can be simple, everyday things.

> *Both abundance and lack exist simultaneously in our lives, as parallel realities. It is always a conscious choice which secret garden we tend.*
>
> —Sarah Ban Breathnach,
> *The Simple Abundance Journal of Gratitude*

8. **Develop a spiritual practice or join a faith community.** Find a community that increases your sense of compassion and positive energy. People who had open-heart surgery were *10 times more likely to survive* if they had a network of support and spiritual faith.

9. **Find mentors.** Like the parable at the end of Chapter One, find the people in your "village" who sustain and support your growth. Spend time with them and watch how they handle tough situations and events. Through observation and conversation they can teach you about their approaches, philosophy, and skills. They don't have fewer challenges and frustrations than the rest of the world; however, they *think about life differently* than people who are consistently cynical and hostile, and therefore their lives are dramatically more positive and satisfying.

   When my son was small I was mentored by his day-care provider. She was a pro. She taught me very effective techniques for putting him to sleep without a hassle, avoid power struggles (parents have power struggles with toddlers all the time), and manage temper tantrums in stores. I didn't have these skills beforehand, but I learned from people who did.

10. **Crisis becomes an opportunity for solidarity without blame.** Once you remove blame from your emotional repertoire, problems become opportunities for teams, leaders, and organizations to bond. Situations that once seemed insurmountable become occasions to build new relationships and deepen existing ones. Self-oriented interests are often suspended in order to achieve overarching goals.

   Without blame, a crisis becomes an occasion to develop new skills and discover previously hidden facets of other people's experiences, training, and capacities. When no one is looking for a scapegoat, a challenge or problem can draw people closer together, rather than moving them further apart. The resulting feelings of achievement and camaraderie reinforce the belief that your colleagues are good people, committed to a worthy cause.

   The opportunity and ability to accomplish a task that no one could achieve alone is an ancient, powerful motivator. It's an intrinsic high that makes work meaningful and motivates people to invest more of themselves in their colleagues, supervisors, and organizations.

   Once blame is banished, errors and snafus create opportunities to experience the endorphins associated with the helper's high.

Positive team effort, minus blame and fear, creates genuine pride in work. Instead of using another person's mistakes for personal gain, individuals pitch in to help others recover and learn. These behaviors create positive reciprocity, a strategy that has been a reliable survival tactic since the first days of human existence.

> *The most natural human response to*
> *catastrophe is to pull together.*
>
> —Thomas Glass,
> John Hopkins School of Public Health

Despite our fears about human nature, studies of natural disasters reveal that unless a population is already troubled (for example, the Rodney King riots in Los Angeles, or Iraqi citizens at the time of the U.S. invasion) crime rates actually drop during catastrophes. The British called this innate reaction "the blitz spirit," which they defined as a self-organized movement of cooperation that developed during the severe and prolonged bombing of England during WW II.

When I visited St. Paul's Cathedral in London, I was moved to tears looking at the photographs of very young and very old men, women, grandfathers, and mothers forming bucket brigades and rescue crews to assist the wounded and save London's most treasured buildings from burning. Imagine: this scenario occurred at a time when the municipal government and police departments were barely functioning! Dr. Thomas Glass believes a "deeply embedded script to react collectively in groups" helps the human race pull together, adapt, and survive.

11. **Look for ways to build positive energy in groups and teams.** This concept is so important that Chapter Eleven is devoted to it. In my work I've learned that those skilled in conflict resolution don't just resolve negative situations and walk away. They replace negativity with positive attitudes, behavior, and energy that bond and sustain people. Skilled resolution renews the source of energy that creates feelings of safety, warmth, respect, positive reciprocity, and the excitement of limitless possibilities. This glue is so powerful that people guard it diligently once they experience it.

Train your brain to stop flooding

If you flood regularly in response to frustration, you'll be sorely disappointed if you expect to never again lose your temper. Like most habits, you can't "flip a switch" and make flooding go away. It takes time and effort to learn new behavior. Facing this issue also takes great courage. Most blaming responses are on automatic pilot, and they are harder to identify and eradicate than you might anticipate.

If you look at the sequence we've been using—thinking triggers emotions, and then emotions shape behaviors—it's likely you'll start from the *bottom and work your way up.* You might first become more aware of negative *behaviors* you'd like to eliminate; then, begin to identify how you *feel* when you're starting to flood; and finally, monitor and choose your *thinking,* or what you say to yourself, when you hit one of your 30 heart-hassles each day.

1. **Use aggressive behavior as a signal.** Your first attempts to stop flooding may come too late to avoid a cascade of adrenaline, hormones, cortisol, and the aggressive behaviors that result. Initially, your insights will occur *after* your body has calmed down enough to start analyzing your behavior. This may not happen until several hours after the incident. Flooding is such a physiological hit that the rational, analytical part of the brain won't be active until later. Don't be discouraged— even noticing your response, and calling it by its medical term is progress! At this juncture, be careful not to get caught in blame's other stinky twin: harsh criticism of yourself. If you beat yourself up for "losing control," you will feel hopeless and give up. Flooding is a *habit.* Reprogramming your mind takes multiple repetitions.

> *There is no finer sensation in life than that which*
> *comes with victory over one's self.*
>
> —Vash Young

Think about being a compassionate witness to your behavior. Identify typical reactions when you flood. How do *you* attempt to alleviate the emotional and physical stress that accompanies flooding? Do you yell, slam doors, throw things, brood, walk away, take long showers, exercise, overeat, withdraw, kick the cat, or pay an extended visit to the local bar? Dr. Richard Shekelle at Northwestern University in Chicago found men (the gender he studied) with higher hostility scores indeed smoke more and consume more alcohol.

We all take actions to alleviate the extreme emotional stress associated with flooding. When individuals aren't informed about flooding or the extreme emotional stress it causes, they engage in unconscious, and relatively ineffective, behaviors to eliminate the powerfully negative feelings.

Blame isn't always accompanied with a red face, bulging veins, and outbursts. The "avoid" forms of blame take on insidious variations, such as exclusion, gossip, undermining, withholding questions, second-guessing motives, rolling eyes, sighing, or silence, rather than speaking on someone's behalf. On which of these behaviors do you rely?

Remember, venting doesn't help. Venting makes it *more* likely that you will flood the next time you face a frustration. The solution is to get your arms around your thinking patterns, and train your brain to think differently. If you flood and lash out against a colleague, direct report, or family member, then use your regret as motivation to reset your responses.

2. **Recognize the feelings associated with flooding.** Your second set of insights may come as you start to tune in to how you *feel* when you flood. Identify your earliest cues that you're headed toward losing control. Is it shallow breathing, a tight gut, tension in your neck and shoulders? How does *your* body manifest the severe emotional stress that is the hallmark of flooding? Do you feel it in your neck, head, arms, or your entire body? Is it pulsing, pounding, tense, anxious, irritable, or frantic? One of my early signals is nausea. Learn to identify the early physiological signals of flooding so you can short circuit the reflexive response.

3. **Identify your inflammatory thinking.** As you become aware of the physiology of flooding you can start identifying the trigger: What are you saying to yourself? Is your thinking inflammatory? What's the message of your inner dialogue? *When you become aware of your thinking you will be able to eliminate the number of times you are at the mercy of blame, flooding, and negative energy.*

4. **Realize you have a choice.** The next step in breaking the blame game is realizing that when you're facing a delay, disappointment, or disagreement you can consciously choose how to react. In your mind's eye you may even see the diagram of the three responses to

frustration we've been using. *As the incident is occurring* you will realize you have choices. Which choice is most useful in achieving your goal?

5. **Enjoy your hard-earned control.** After you've gained control of thinking, and faced down many frustrations without blame, your automatic responses will take less conscious effort.

Mastering these thinking patterns enhances relationships, and promotes fiscal strength, pleasant emotions, and resilient health.

Identify your targets and triggers

Identifying the people and groups you target is a useful step in ending habits of blame. You might start by becoming conscious of the times you "take the bait" and join others in ridiculing individuals or groups. Be brutally honest about who you blame when your life, work, or project hits a barrier.

If you can't think of anyone you blame, look at your emotional reactions: with whom do you overreact? Who pushes your buttons? Which groups or people make you steamy? Who is the butt of your jokes and put-downs?

Do you feel antagonistic toward men, women, different occupations, different ethnicities, immigrants, southerners, rich, poor, tree huggers, bad drivers, people from the East Coast, young people, seniors?

Who do you target at work?

At work, who do you consistently avoid or enjoy ridiculing? Common workplace targets include new hires, senior employees, colleagues, bosses, upper management, unions, temps, human resources, IT, other departments, other plants, and so on.

If you work in a corporation, you or your colleagues might scapegoat engineering, purchasing, operations, sales, the executive team, the stockholders, your president, CFO, the board, suppliers, customer services, shipping, service, operators, technicians, administration, OSHA, quality control, your parent company, or another plant or shift.

Targeted groups in government or social services include politicians, clients, citizens, families, youth, Republicans, Democrats, corporations, commissioners, legislators, the mayor, PACs, lobbyists, city council, or the governor.

If you work in a college or university, targets are often deans, commissioners, students, faculty, tenured professors, teaching assistants, or other schools, disciplines, or departments.

The list is endless. When do you find yourself getting energy from self-righteous indignation and contempt? Is the majority of your humor based on put-downs of another group or person? When do you talk about others in denigrating ways? What groups or departments are on the receiving end of your blame? When do you and your colleagues use attacks on others as a form of entertainment?

Be honest. This thinking is almost universal. Use the space below to list the groups or people that come to mind. You'll use these lists in Chapter Seven.

Again, if no person or group comes to mind, think about your emotions. When you flood, who's on the receiving end? Who do you resent? Who makes you mad? What people or groups are on your list of pet peeves?

_____

_____

_____

_____

_____

_____

Who do you target in your personal life?

Many of my clients report that they manage their anger and irritability quite well at work; however, their behavior at home is an entirely different story. This isn't unusual. Many people are more polite and tolerant at work than at home.

For many, emotional meltdowns occur at the end of the working day, when they face the second wave of daily demands—the drain of maintaining a home and attending to the needs and idiosyncrasies of partners, pets, children, meals, laundry, bills, errands, and neighbors—at a time when their physical and emotional stamina has been depleted.

Although flooding at home may seem less costly than flooding at work, the residue is just as damaging, if not more so. The medical data we covered in Chapter Two is clear—relationships at home have the power to either make us sick or help us heal.

If you're flooding with your children, you're damaging ties to loved ones who can either be a source of pride and intimacy, or bring your life (and perhaps your career) to its knees. There are unlimited variations of both passive and aggressive responses to adult flooding that children engage in. Cutting, depression, truancy, running away, eating disorders, sexual promiscuity, and chemical dependency are only a few of the ways children create paybacks for emotional attacks and outbursts from their parents. I've worked with more than one CEO who was struggling with variations of this scenario.

In your personal life, do you blame your children, brothers, a spouse, an ex-spouse, parents, a boyfriend, neighbors, sisters, the government, teachers, a girlfriend, coaches, referees, players, racial or ethnic groups, liberals or conservatives, car mechanic, plumber, gays or straights? Who do you make fun of?

_____

_____

_____

_____

_____

_____

Situational stress

Some people don't target specific individuals or groups. They are more vulnerable to flooding and negativity when they face specific, stressful situations. Do you flood when flights are late, when other drivers cut you off, while preparing your taxes or paying bills, at sport events, waiting in lines, facing the mini-rebellions of children, when you read the stock market report or watch the news? Do you have a particular weakness for flooding when technology fails in the forms of computers losing data, cars stalling, batteries going dead, or software that won't integrate with other systems?

> *The maelstrom of fatherhood is a chance to show grace under real pressure, to be cool despite the chaos of your son's room.*
>
> *That's something that's worth a fellow's time.*
>
> —Hugh O'Neill
>
> Author of *A Man Called Daddy*

Jot down the situations or places where you feel intense irritability, or feel yourself beginning to flood. Again, you'll use this list in Chapter Seven.

Six ways to extinguish inflammatory thinking

Many people have contributed to the research on cognitive therapy and negative self-talk. Among the most well-known are psychologists Kenneth Burns and Martin Seligman. Their books helped me develop my early insights into the power of thinking to shape moods and behavior.

As you begin to get conscious of your patterns you can short-circuit the flooding response by paying attention to how you think. When you feel yourself starting to flood, use any of the following techniques. For now, choose one or two that you find the most appealing. Practice it for a few weeks and then return to these pages and adopt additional strategies.

1. When you start feeling tense ask, "What am I saying to myself? Is it helping me?" If your thinking is making you anxious or upset, ask yourself one following questions.

2. Ask, "What are the facts? Is there a "baby in the back seat?" Why might this problem exist?" Give yourself the assignment of generating

multiple scenarios of why *reasonable* people might be behaving in this manner. This technique keeps you in the cortex, the problem-solving center of the brain.

For instance, if someone is late for a business meeting, generate all the possible reasons for his or her delay. It's an interesting way to entertain yourself and you can check the accuracy of your speculations when they arrive. You won't have to do this for long—again, it's a technique to replace reflexive aggression with new habits of curiosity and concern.

3. Ask yourself, "What's reasonable and realistic?" It's not necessary to adopt a habit of forced optimism—in some studies optimism was found to be a less useful coping mechanism than pessimism. But what about realism? What's *reasonable*? This question will counter our tendency to catastrophize or inflame a crisis or stressor. Catastrophizing is defined as the mental rehearsal of the all the things that can go wrong following a particular event. It's a surefire way to crank up anxiety and dread. Instead, ask yourself, "What's reasonable?"

4. Finishing the following phrase three times is another anti-inflammatory trick: "At least it's not..." This exercise can become a source of black humor and a nutty coping mechanism for yourself and your group. "Well, my new workspace is in the middle of the route to the bathroom, but at least I'm not in the stairwell!" "My computer crashed but at least I wasn't injured!" "The coffee pot is empty again but at least my coffee mug is now full." Focus on what's *there*, not what's lacking. These are ridiculous responses. However, that's precisely why they short-circuit flooding and indignation.

I heard a psychologist explain that he and his family (his wife and two teenager children) travel across the state of Iowa—on bicycles—in July. They join a fundraising event that requires they sleep in tents and, on occasion, use cornfields for bathrooms.

He explained that this was a great bonding experience for his family, but it also had another, unanticipated, benefit. It *lowered* the bar of what his family considered essential.

A few months after his last trip he was traveling for business and his flight was delayed by a mechanical problem that developed after the plane had taxied away from the gate. When the captain announced that the passengers would not be allowed to disembark until the problem was resolved, *everyone* but the psychologist flooded.

He sank back into his seat and said, "Well, at least we have ice water. At least there are multiple toilets. At least I'm sitting in a comfortable, air-conditioned environment in a padded chair with something to read. "At least it's not," is the *opposite* of inflammatory thinking.

5. Whatever you focus on expands in your mind. During rush-hour traffic people are often tailgating and abruptly changing lanes. Many times, when I'm in this situation I can feel myself starting to get tense. Shifting my attention to the people who *aren't* driving that way is an effective antidote. There are *lots* of people who still drive "the old-fashioned way." I don't lose track of what the hotheads are doing, but I reduce my stress by not obsessing about their behavior.

During a presentation of this material to a group of CEOs one of them blurted out, "How am I supposed to stop flooding?! The other day I was the driver for my carpool. I was in the fast lane and the person in front of me was going *below* the speed limit! What am I supposed to say to myself about that?"

I imagined his poor passengers, trying to catch a few more minutes of shuteye or finish paperwork, and their driver is blowing his cool at the pace of the preceding driver. What a waste of a pleasant mood and tranquility. I suggested he shift his attention to *anything* else: classical music, the book his colleague was reading, a pressing issue at work.

In a sense, the nature of our thinking is determined by our intentions. If I want to search for stupidity, my brain will comply. If I realize the price I'm paying for this nearly invisible decision, I can shift my thinking and other realities will dominate my thoughts.

For a detailed example of how our intentions shape data see "Transforming the Enemy" in the appendix. It highlights the reality that when we want to see someone as deserving of our contempt, we selectively filter data to support our intention, even as we review the "facts."

6. There is one sentence that I find particularly effective when I'm trying not to flood. I say to myself, "You can be effective or self-righteous; pick one." Before I changed phone services, I used this phrase frequently while waiting an endless amount of time for someone to answer a service call. Although I knew the wait was unreasonable I also knew that if I became irritable and indignant while I waited, when customer service finally answered my call, I would not be able to do the complex thinking that was necessary to solve my problem.

It's especially hard not to flood when we feel we've earned a good outburst. Last year I struggled with holding my anger at bay during my third trip to Kinko's to pick up material I needed for a Monday morning meeting. Kinko's was printing off a disk and, on my first and second trips to pick up the order, which occurred over the weekend, I discovered that the computer had dropped data off the copies. At first I was able to retain my calm with relative ease. However, when I found the error again, on my *third* trip—the morning of the meeting— while dealing with yet *another* store manager, I had to struggle to hold back my anger. By then I *deserved* a good outburst! Yet at a rational level I knew the costs I would incur by taking my frustrations out on the hapless manager. It was more important to fix the problem and have the materials I needed.

Working with their computer expert, the third store manager identified the reason for the recurring errors, and the manager agreed to my request to give me the materials at no cost. As I got into my car I patted myself on the back for my self-control, drove 10 minutes toward the site of the meeting, and realized I had left my calendar with the directions, contact information, and phone numbers for the meeting— *at Kinko's!*

I felt like an idiot. However, when I called the manager on my cell phone and asked him to find my calendar and read me the directions I was incredibly grateful that I had treated him with respect. He responded to my request immediately and sounded relieved that he could return a favor.

Kinko's employees, working with a computer with which they were unfamiliar, had made a series of mistakes. I held them accountable but I did it with warmth. Fifteen minutes later, *I* made a significant error. However, this is where positive reciprocity works its magic. Because I hadn't used Kinko's errors to make a scene, the manager kindly went out of his way to help me out of a bind. Reciprocity is a valuable, reliable principle, and we'll explore it in detail in the next chapter.

In order to stay in positive energy, you don't have to walk around thinking, *"Isn't everyone wonderful?!"* In fact, the opposite is a more effective approach. *We're all flawed.* So what's the advantage of flooding?

Unless you are in imminent physical danger, the reason you are flooding is not because of the event, but because of your *thinking*.

Drag yourself back to neutral and ask yourself again, "What could be rational reasons for the other person's behavior?" This assignment forces your brain to use the cortex.

EASE: Calming a flooded employee or customer

In the beginning of your transition to blame-free thinking, your cronies and friends will still invite you to join them in denigrating another person or group. If you've been susceptible to blaming others in the past, there will be moments when others will expect you to ridicule a well-worn scapegoat, and they will be surprised if you no longer join in. Over time, people will learn that you no longer "take the bait" when they try to gain your support for attributing the cause of frustration to other people's personalities.

You can tell people directly that you've made a decision to stop blaming. Or, if you prefer, you can make the transition so seamless and effortless that others won't even notice that you no longer join in to ridicule a target. Your supervisor, colleagues, and direct reports may be puzzled that you seem more laid back, fun, and warm, but they won't be able to pinpoint the exact nature of your change.

Revisiting the case of the angry police officer

We can quickly see the advantages of sidestepping an invitation to blame someone by returning to the situation of the police officer in Chapter Five. That scenario is a perfect example of a direct report setting up his supervisor to blame his bosses' boss. *Very* tempting.

A quick review of the facts: While I was working in Wisconsin with police departments, three officers were paged out of the room to respond to a citizen who had barricaded himself in an apartment with a small arsenal of guns and was threatening to kill himself or anyone who came close. With great skill and courage, the officers were able to convince the gunman to surrender and he was taken to jail.

Imagine that one of the three officers later returns to his desk and finds a memo from the mayor denying his department's request for bulletproof vests. The officer, who is already flooded from the high-risk assignment, reacts to the memo and storms into his chief's office to blast the mayor.

In Chapter Five, the chief surrendered to the temptation of attributing the department's problems by targeting an absent person. The chief doesn't realize the price he'll pay for his lack of integrity.

Instead of this negative scenario, let's see how the chief can calm his officer, bond with him, preserve his pride in the organization, and move toward solving the problem. This is the reflective, problem-solving orientation at its best.

The technique is called "EASE." and it is very effective. It utilizes the same principles that Michael and Julie Weisser used intuitively when they defused the anger and hatred of the KKK's Grand Dragon, Larry Trapp. A hard-headed search for solutions combined with warmth and appreciation is an irresistible response to someone who is bent on blaming another person or group for his or her frustration.

You'll find that when you use this technique with someone who is flooded, he or she will drop the energy of negativity in a heartbeat for a chance to feel the calming energy of genuine appreciation.

There are four steps to EASE: **E**mpathy, **A**ppreciation, **S**earch for Solutions, and **E**xplore. First you'll have an opportunity to apply EASE to the chief's situation. Following that exercise, you can script out a response to a familiar pattern of blame from your work.

1. Be empathic to the frustration.

First, the chief should react to the reality of the officer's situation. He can acknowledge that returning from a dangerous run and finding a memo that denies crucial safety equipment is demoralizing. The chief can understand that the officer's reaction makes sense. The chief's direct report is having strong, negative reactions because he's concluded that his safety is not important to administration.

Empathy is identifying and understanding another person's feelings. It does *not* mean you have to agree with them, although you may. Genuine empathy requires feeling another person's expressed and unexpressed emotions, which are almost always reasonable, *given their worldview.* You may have a different perspective, but you will be more effective if you acknowledge his or hers first.

Acknowledging another person's frustration is the first step toward helping them regain control of their emotions. In my experience, most people become more agitated and aggressive when they feel their concerns have been dismissed or minimized. Listening and empathizing produces the opposite result.

Imagine you are the chief of police, and Mike, the officer, has returned from a dangerous assignment and is justifiably frustrated about finding a memo denying needed equipment. Acknowledge his frustration. How would you agree with the officer that his frustration is understandable given his world view?

_____

_____

_____

_____

_____

2. State your appreciation for his or her commitment, expertise, and efforts.

Many times employees go to a supervisor or colleague and say, "I have to vent." A detailed narrative of how they overcame a series of unpreventable barriers to complete a task almost always follows this statement.

However, as we've already established, venting isn't an effective anti-dote for flooding or negative emotions. Therapists no longer give their clients pillows and plastic bats to beat out their anger and frustrations. Venting and aggression actually reinforce the circuitry associated with flooding and predisposes people to future expressions of anger—making it _more_ likely a flooding response will occur.

It's more effective to change your thinking patterns and eliminate the problem, rather than to manage it after it's occurred. Once we've flooded, the chemicals have already entered the circulatory system.

Helping a colleague or customer change their physiology into the energy of appreciation is one of the most effective ways to alleviate the discomfort that accompanies flooding. Remember the heart rhythm of appreciation from Chapter One? By shifting the emotional tone of the conversation from hostility to appreciation, you can help your colleague or customer regain their feelings of well-being by acknowledging the strength of their commitment to solving the problem.

The chief has a perfect opportunity to help his officer make this shift. He could ask for details about how they disarmed the resident. The chief could acknowledge and commend his officers' expertise in handling the incident. The three officers convinced the citizen to surrender—an act that took tremendous skill.

I've used this technique multiple times, and I get the same results that the Weissers received from the Grand Dragon, Larry Trapp. Like Larry, my clients drop their hostility for a chance to bask in the positive feelings of having someone recognize and respect their intentions and contributions.

Again, put yourself in the shoes of the chief. What could he say that might motivate the officer to drop his anger in exchange for the opportunity to hear someone pay tribute to his commitment, service, and professionalism?

---

3. Speculate about reasons.

The shift to reflective thinking will be automatic if the chief speculates about the mayor or city council's rationale. What "baby" might they have in the back seat of *their* car?

The chief can take this step even if he doesn't know the reason or agree with the city council's conclusion. At this juncture, it's just important he takes the focus off the decision-maker and put it solidly on the situation. Speculate—the options are limitless. Perhaps the city council is facing a budget shortfall. Maybe they need information about the cost savings associated with vests. Perhaps they are misinformed about the efficacy of the vests. Maybe they are waiting for a substantial uniform expenditure in the next fiscal cycle. How would you segue the officer towards more reflective thinking?

_____

_____

_____

_____

_____

4. Explore next steps.

By addressing the situation in this manner, the chief has acknowledged that there is a problem, and he has bonded with his direct report without incriminating the mayor. He has taken steps to ensure his officer is thinking about the problem rationally. Now, the chief has to address the problem and, if possible, identify a specific, measurable next step.

The chief could make several suggestions: they could invite the mayor to their next staff meeting to discuss options and barriers, they could make an appointment to see her, or the chief could simply pick up the phone. Perhaps they need to collect data for the mayor to take to the city council on the effectiveness of the vests. Or maybe the chief already knows the situation is not worth pursing with administration. In that case, the next step might be looking for alternative sources of funding.

This last step is reassuring to a direct report. It's clear the supervisor is more than talk. In most cases, direct reports have no choice but to rely on their supervisor's willingness to elevate and act on problems that are important to staff.

Again, take a few minutes to imagine and record a reasonable next step for the chief and his officer.

_____

_____

_____

_____

_____

_____

If you want to eliminate the hazards of blame from your life, your ability and willingness to open the dialogue—even in awkward situations— is critical. I think this was one of the reasons for the latter half of Einstein's famous quote, "It takes a touch of genius, and a lot of courage to move in the opposite direction."

In your words

Following is an opportunity to apply these insights to a situation in *your* life. Imagine an ongoing frustration for you, your direct reports, colleagues, or customers that often results in someone storming into your work area flooded and intent on "venting." Identify a legitimate frustration, and a typical person or group who gets targeted. If nothing at work comes to mind, address a situation in your family.

_____

_____

_____

_____

_____

1. **How could you bond through the use of *empathy*—a stated understanding of the frustrations the other person is feeling?**

Again, listen for the hurt and wounded pride under the anger. Do this *without* agreeing that the cause of their frustration is a person, department, or group.

_____

_____

_____

_____

_____

_____

2. Write two or three statements you could make in *appreciation* of the person or his or her efforts.

You might comment on level of expertise, desire to resolve the frustration, the investment they have in work, or more specifically, the actions they've already taken to resolve the problem before coming to you. If you let yourself *feel* the other person's passion, you may notice that underneath anger often lays a deeply felt desire for things to run more smoothly, with fewer complications. What words would *you* use to comment on their commitment, talent, and investment in work?

_____

_____

_____

_____

_____

_____

3. What "babies" (constraints, demands, pressures) might be in the back seat of the targeted party?

What legitimate pressures could cause the other parties' behavior? Consider budget shortfalls; lack of time, resources, or staff; interruptions; illness; market pressures; safety constraints; shipping problems; lack of information; operation limitations; bottlenecks; misunderstandings, lost data, and so on.

At this step, I think of myself as the mythical Sherlock Holmes: dispassionate, analytical, and open to any possibility or surprise. The main goal in step three is to replace negative assumptions and judgments with curiosity and concern. Assume that the other party is reasonable and invested in doing a good job. Consider that the source of your problem might be in the situation or in your systems. We'll cover this possibility in more detail in Chapter Eight.

> Workplace problems are often the result
> of incompatible performance measures.

If I'm in sales and my quarterly bonus is based on the number of orders I generate, then I'll have little concern for the impact on operations and I'll dismiss their frustrations as lack of imagination, or an unwillingness to go the extra mile for a customer. However, if I understand their performance measures, I'll see that their behavior *is* reasonable, given the evaluation criteria that will be used to evaluate their performance, and perhaps base *their* compensation, at year-end. If the problem seems serious, I might even raise the issue that performance measures are causing tension between departments. This is actually quite common, but it is rarely diagnosed because employees and leaders are often focused on personalities, rather than policies, as the source of the problem.

Brainstorm the known or possible *constraints and pressures* of the other party in the situation you've identified.

_____

_____

_____

_____

_____

4. **What *actions* might your direct report, colleague, or family member take to open the dialogue or problem-solve?**

What would make a reasonable first step? Data collection, a conversation, arranging a cross-functional meeting? Identify three or four.

_____

_____

_____

_____

_____

_____

The alternatives to blame take skill and courage, but they are simple and effective, they are easily within reach, and *they can become just as automatic as blame and contempt.* Bonding and bridging to other people and departments through empathy and appreciation has multiple advantages to your body, profitability, retention, morale, pride, productivity, and effectiveness. Once the energy of appreciation takes hold of an organization, the possibilities for growth and resilience are almost limitless. When many minds combine for the common good their accomplishments are breathtaking.

Saving your time and sanity

Think back to the examples in Chapter Four, the "The shut-out employee," or "The defiant power plant operators," where either party could have broken a stalemate with innocent questions and saved themselves frustration and embarrassment.

People don't reach out to clarify their perceptions because they fear they will make a moderately troubled situation worse. In Chapter Nine you'll learn a way to open the dialogue that is both safe and powerful.

Never again will you have to wonder what someone's behavior means. Rather than resorting to silent and inaccurate speculations, you will ask for his or her help in understanding his or her actions, and you will do it in a way that entices him or her to join you on a hardheaded search for solutions.

Chapter Seven

If I'm Not Part
of the Problem,
There Is No Solution:
Breaking Cycles of Contempt

Is there one word that can guide you for your whole life?
Yes. It is reciprocity.

—Confucius

At a local bakery an employee took my order for a dozen bagels, brought a handful to the counter, and set to work slicing them. Her colleague, who was momentarily unoccupied, glanced at the pile, and without comment pitched in to help.

A few minutes later, as the second woman rang up my order I commented on her good-natured assistance and asked if lending a hand was something her company promoted. "No," she said shyly, "not really. And, I don't help everyone," she was quick to add. "I just help people who help me."

Although most people don't recognize the word "reciprocity," almost everyone lives by its principles. Reciprocity, the natural tendency to match the other party's behavior, is a fascinating phenomenon to observe. It quietly influences your success, resiliency, and relationships. You are on the receiving end of thousands of acts of reciprocal behavior, which are based on your initial actions. These exchanges have been accruing throughout your life.

Once you understand this, you will be able to put reciprocity to work, and many previously puzzling behaviors will suddenly make sense. In formal studies of international conflict, reciprocity is considered one of the most reliable predictors of human behavior.

Many people have told me that after they've been introduced to the concept of reciprocity and completed the following exercises, they've dramatically changed their behavior. For the first time they understood *why* the negative assumptions of others almost *guarantees* negative outcomes. They also realize that by changing their views of difficult situations they are able to change their outcomes. The true story, "Transforming the Enemy," which is in the appendix, describes how I changed my behavior and triggered a shift in a situation that had troubled me for seven years.

Dr. John Gottman, a psychologist at the University of Washington, studied reciprocity in his psychology laboratory for more than 20 years. By collecting biofeedback data on couples discussing hot-button issues in their relationships, Gottman was able to predict the outcome of tense conversations with 96-percent accuracy. If the initiator opened the conversation with a harsh setup, his or her partner flooded with 96-percent reliability. When the initiator opened the conversation with appreciation and warmth, the conversation ended on that note, almost invariably. That means that *only 4 percent of the time did a participant* not *match the emotional tone of his or her partner.*

This is one of the reasons why contempt, backstabbing, and ridicule are self-defeating. When we succumb to those emotions and behaviors the recipient mirrors our behavior. We experience a jolt of indignation and righteousness as our worst fears about the other party are confirmed. However, we have postponed, or lost, the opportunity to solve the problem.

Once you understand reciprocity, you will be able to see it operating flawlessly in every organization, workplace, and society.

Negative reciprocity is reliable and predictable

Some forms of reciprocity are very subtle. Others are massive and impossible to miss. Examples include:

▷ Hoarding resources or knowledge when others hoard theirs.

▷ Returning an insult to a colleague or stranger.

▷ Ignoring an indifferent coworker.

▷ Making obscene gestures to an aggressive driver.

▷ Sending dinner invitations to an individual who never returns the overture.

▷ Gossiping about someone who is spreading rumors about you.

▷ Curtailing employee privileges after a strike.

▷ Purposely running work orders incorrectly after privileges are curtailed.

▷ Sabotaging computer systems after being callously fired.

▷ Voting to strike after benefit or salary contractions.

▷ Matching or exceeding another country's threats, assaults, invasions, or armament.

Positive reciprocity is reliable and predictable

▷ Sharing resources or knowledge when others share theirs.

▷ Grasping the offered handshake.

▷ Repaying a kindness from a colleague or stranger.

▷ Standing up for someone who has defended you.

▷ Leaving an extravagant tip for an outstanding waiter or waitress.

▷ Lending a tool to a helpful neighbor.

▷ Buying lunch with a coworker.

▷ Remembering the anniversaries or birthdays of someone who faithfully remembers yours.

▷ Distributing bonuses for outstanding performance.

▷ Speaking well of a company that laid you off with expressed regret and respect.

▷ Employees agreeing to reductions in benefits or compensation after management has reduced theirs.

▷ Matching another country's reduction of threats, assaults, invasions, or arms.

Christmas morning Marine

My 88-year-old father, an American Marine in the Pacific Islands during World War II, told me a story about the tenacity of reciprocity. On Christmas morning his battalion was ordered to storm a small island near Australia that was occupied by Japanese troops. The plan was to proceed up the beach, push back the first line of defense, return to the shore, and circle the edge of the island to move behind the Japanese artillery.

As they returned to the beach after their first wave, and in the midst of chaos and confusion, he heard the disconcerting sound of a female's voice ringing out, "Hey, Yank! Do you want a cup of coffee?" He turned and saw that at the edge of the beach were two civilians from the Australian Salvation Army setting up a booth to distribute coffee.

In a small but symbolic gesture of reciprocity, they were thanking the Marines for their willingness to protect Australia on Christmas morning.

However, the circle of reciprocity turned again. Just before the war ended, my father, suffering from malaria, was on leave in California. As he finished his meal in a diner he noticed two Australian Salvation Army workers eating breakfast, and without a word, he paid for their meals as he left.

The act of kindness from the Australian Salvation Army prompted my him to write them a thank-you letter last Christmas—an example of the innate desire to reciprocate that stretched over 60 years.

Hostility shows

When our feelings toward others are positive, we publicly show our warmth. Our fondness and affection for another person or group is obvious.

However, when our feelings for another person or group are negative, we believe that we can successfully hide our attitudes of superiority, contempt, or indifference. Despite our hopes (or illusions), negative feelings toward others are not well-concealed.

The author and medical doctor, Deepak Chopra, wrote, "Our hostility, fear, mistrust, and insecurity are not as deeply seated as our ego would like to believe." When we are hostile or insecure we clearly communicate these emotions. In this chapter you will see that both positive and negative assumptions about other people or groups are transparent and self-fulfilling.

Reciprocity flows: Cycles of Contempt and Courage

Drawing Cycles of Contempt and Courage, circular flowcharts of positive and negative reciprocity, is a quick and powerful way to look at how the initiator's behavior is seen, interpreted, and returned by the receiver. During my seminars, participants are given an opportunity to draw both positive and negative cycles addressing situations from their personal or professional lives. More than once, participants have been so impressed by their insights that they have taken their findings back to their workplace (or family) and used them to open discussions.

We'll look first at four Cycles of Contempt drawn by workshop participants. Then you'll see vastly different outcomes when these same participants make a second attempt to solve their problems with Cycles of Courage.

Cycles of Contempt are inflammatory and reflexive

In negative cycles we assume that the cause of our frustration is the personality of another party—they are selfish, stupid, or clueless. You'll see that this reflexive, inflammatory reaction, and subsequent behavior triggers a reciprocal response from the other person. The other party's (person or group's) damaging behavior validates the original negative assumption.

When we draw Cycles, we start by identifying a situation that the participant would like to improve. Then the participant records the *facts* without embellishment or speculation. In cycles of contempt I ask them to use reflexive blaming *thinking*, assuming the other party's personality is the cause of the problem. The other person or group is *unreasonable*, that's why this problem exists!

In the third step, participants record their *behavior* based on their thinking. This behavior is always some form of attack and avoid. They might be harsh, short tempered, abrupt, irritable, or demanding. He or she might nag, withdraw, or send critical e-mails that are copied to others, or denigrate the other party behind their back.

In Cycles, the diagrams also include the reactions of the other party. At step four the initiator has to put themselves in the other person's shoes and imagines *how their behavior looks* to the other party. What do they see or hear? At this point most people realize how judgmental and harsh their behavior appears to others.

Given his or her behavior, the initiator speculates how the other person might view him or her as a person. This step is a good test of empathy. Can the initiator imagine what the other person will *think* of him or her, based on his or her behavior?

In Cycles of Contempt the recipient's *behavior* is often as negative, or more so, than the initiator's. How will the recipient behave based upon what he or she thinks of the initiator?

What does the initiator *observe?* Typically, it confirms his or her original negative assumption.

Let's move to four examples of Cycles of Contempt, followed by four Cycles of Courage, and these powerful but subtle exchanges will become clear.

A Cycle of Contempt:
Project managers and architects

Lenore was a project manager (PM) at a large, highly respected property management and construction company. Within her organization there had been ongoing tension between the project managers who oversaw site construction, and the architects, who created the blueprints on which the project managers relied.

The project managers were held accountable for budget and they worked hard to complete their projects at or below their estimates. Fiscal conservatism was one of their company's selling points, and a source of pride for the project managers.

Lenore's, as a project manager, thought the architects lived in a world of fantasy, oblivious to the day-to-day realities of material and budget constraints. The PMs felt the architects wasted time and money designing features that were aesthetic, but unnecessary and expensive.

Lenore drew a Cycle of Contempt (Figure 10) to address the ongoing tension. She started her cycle with the facts:

1. Frustration: "The architects' designs are over budget."

As per the assignment, she used negative, reflexive thinking and blamed the personalities of the architects for the problem. It wasn't difficult for her to make her next statement—it was an opinion that was frequently expressed among the project managers.

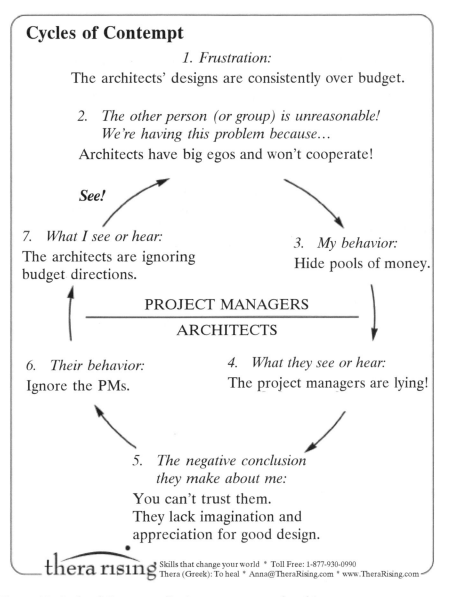

Cycles of Contempt

1. Frustration:
The architects' designs are consistently over budget.

2. *The other person (or group) is unreasonable!
We're having this problem because…*
Architects have big egos and won't cooperate!

See!

7. *What I see or hear:*
The architects are ignoring
budget directions.

3. *My behavior:*
Hide pools of money.

PROJECT MANAGERS

ARCHITECTS

6. *Their behavior:*
Ignore the PMs.

4. *What they see or hear:*
The project managers are lying!

5. *The negative conclusion
they make about me:*
You can't trust them.
They lack imagination and
appreciation for good design.

thera rising Skills that change your world * Toll Free: 1-877-930-0990
Thera (Greek): To heal * Anna@TheraRising.com * www.TheraRising.com

Figure 10. Cycle of Contempt: Project managers and architects

2. Negative, reflexive assumption: "Architects have big egos and won't cooperate!"

3. My behavior: She wrote down the informal policy among the project managers, "Hide pools of money." Because the PMs expected overages in the architect's designs they purposely misrepresented the total amount of resources they had at their disposal.

When Lenore went underneath the horizontal line, she crossed into the world of the architects and had to put herself in their shoes.

4. What they see or hear: Lenore had to guess how the architects viewed the project managers' behavior. After pondering this situation from the architects' perspective she wrote, "The project managers are lying!" Perhaps newly hired architects wouldn't suspect discrepancies in the budget figures during their first project, but by the third or fourth building they would have realized that the budgets were consistently larger than the project managers had indicated at the onset.

Lenore looked at her cycle for a few moments. Again, she put herself in the shoes of the architects and began thinking out-loud, "If I were an architect and I knew that the PMs were consistently misrepresenting budget parameters, how would I view them?

5. The negative conclusion they make about me: She wrote, "You can't trust the project managers. They lack imagination and appreciation for good design."

Having developed an understanding of the architects' conclusions concerning the PMs, Lenore continued to the next question.

6. Their behavior: She asked herself, "What would the architects do to retailiate for the dishonesty of the project managers?"

"Ignore the PMs," she wrote. She started laughing—for the first time she realized how the two groups had created a ludicrous, self-fulfilling power struggle.

When Lenore moved back above the horizontal line in her Cycle of Contempt she was back in the world of the project managers.

7. What I see or hear: She wrote, "The architects are *ignoring* budget directions!" When the architects dismissed the budget concerns of the project managers they came full circle, validating the PMs' negative assumptions.

This is the most tricky, fascinating, heartbreaking, and valuable part of the Cycle of Contempt. When the project managers saw the architects ignoring their budget advice it validated the PMs' beliefs that the architects weren't team players. The PMs concluded that the architects were aloof and ignorant about the fiscal aspects of their work. Their worst fears were confirmed and they felt justified in continuing to denigrate the architect's within their group and to withholding the actual budget parameters. It's obvious that the project managers' *thinking* was part of the perpetual tension and mistrust between the groups.

Cycles validate the negative opinions of *both* groups. Unless someone stepped out of the reoccurring cycle of negative reciprocity, the architects would continue to view the project managers as tiresome, but necessary, boneheads.

Cycles of Courage are analytical and reflective

In contrast, Cycles of Courage assume that the other person or group is *reasonable*. They might lack skill, insight, or self-confidence, however, *so might I*. In Cycles of Courage, we use the same thinking pattern as the "baby in the back" seat example—we assume that something in the *situation* is driving the other person's behavior.

These examples are called Cycles of Courage because, as you'll see, they take more skill and courage. Attacking the other person behind his or her back or avoiding them doesn't take much nerve. When we refuse to paint the other party with the broad brush of contempt, or when we consider that the other party is more like us than not, we are inclined to open a dialogue with them. Skill and courage enter the picture. In Chapter Nine we'll explore a technique that allows you to take this step with grace and confidence, even in the most awkward situations.

Once you understand reciprocity you'll know that it's very likely you can change a Cycle of Contempt by changing your thinking. A shift in thinking almost always alters the way people behave, which triggers a more positive response from the other party.

A Cycle of Courage:
Project managers and architects

When Lenore returned to the exercise to address the same situation with more reflective thinking (Figure 11), she realized that she had the power to end the standoff between the two groups.

In Cycles of Courage, participants use the reflective thinking pattern. What if the perpetual tension over the budget *wasn't* caused by the personalities of the architects? What else could it be? Again, this is similar to

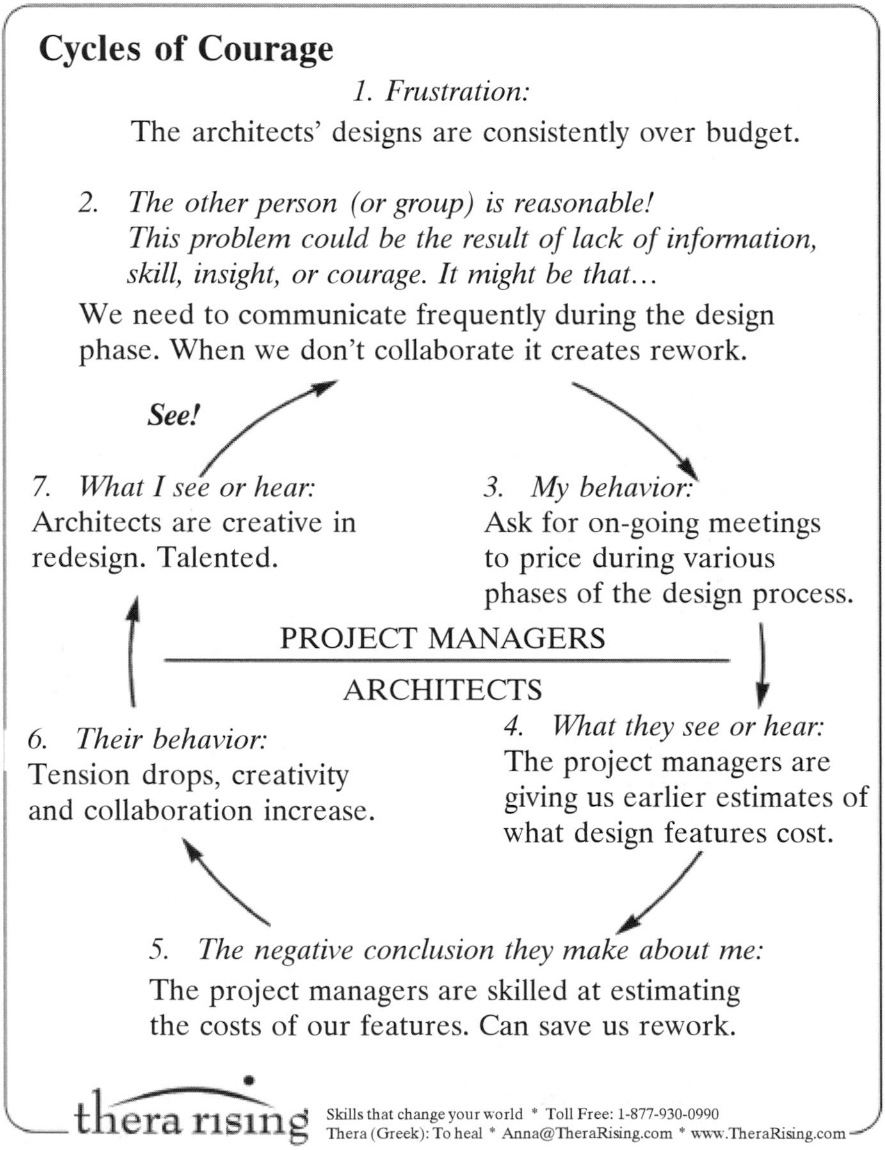

Cycles of Courage

1. Frustration:
The architects' designs are consistently over budget.

2. *The other person (or group) is reasonable!*
    This problem could be the result of lack of information,
    skill, insight, or courage. It might be that...
    We need to communicate frequently during the design phase. When we don't collaborate it creates rework.

See!

7. *What I see or hear:*
    Architects are creative in redesign. Talented.

3. *My behavior:*
    Ask for on-going meetings to price during various phases of the design process.

PROJECT MANAGERS
ARCHITECTS

6. *Their behavior:*
    Tension drops, creativity and collaboration increase.

4. *What they see or hear:*
    The project managers are giving us earlier estimates of what design features cost.

5. *The negative conclusion they make about me:*
    The project managers are skilled at estimating the costs of our features. Can save us rework.

thera rising
Skills that change your world * Toll Free: 1-877-930-0990
Thera (Greek): To heal * Anna@TheraRising.com * www.TheraRising.com

Figure 11. Cycle of Courage: Project managers and architects

giving your brain the new command: why would a *reasonable* person behave in this manner? Are there system problems between the two groups? Are they working off different sets of data? Are they trying to please different clients or supervisors? Are their bonuses based on criteria that pit the project managers and architects against each other? Are there incompatible performance measures between the two groups?

When Lenore considered situational possibilities she realized she was facing a system problem. The architects *weren't* too egotistical or temperamental to worry about budget. The problem was too much interdependent work was being done in isolation. The architects worked independently to draw up blueprints and then delivered their designs to the project managers for pricing. To resolve this issue they needed to fix the *process* (the steps and sequence) they used to accomplish their joint task: a building that would meet or exceed customer expectations. The key players needed to create opportunities to collaborate during the process and incorporate each other's expertise into the design.

In Cycles of Courage, when participants return to their problem, they don't change the basic facts of the frustration, they change how they think about the source of the problem. Lenore wrote again:

#1. "The architect's designs are consistently over budget."

In responding to **#2**, her thinking was more reflective and less inflammatory: "We need to communicate frequently during the design phase. When we don't collaborate it creates rework." As her thinking changed, Lenore's behavior changed.

For **#3** (My behavior), she wrote, "Ask for ongoing meetings to price during phases of the design process."

How would the architects view the shift? When Lenore went underneath the horizontal line she put herself in the architects' shoes and responded to **#4** from their perspective: "The project managers are giving us earlier estimates of what design features cost."

For **#5** (Their thinking), she wrote, "The project managers are skilled at estimating the costs of our features and can save us rework."

For **#6** (The architect's behavior), Lenore wrote, "Tension drops, creativity and collaboration increase."

When Lenore went above the horizontal line she resumed her role as a project manager.

After **#7** ("What the project managers see"), Lenore wrote, "Architects are creative in redesign. Talented. See! They *are* reasonable!"

Lenore realized that if the two groups created more opportunities for dialogue and discussion during the design phase, two very desirable things would occur. The architects would become more knowledgeable about the costs associated with building their prized features, and the project managers would learn more about why the architects were reluctant to build the same basic design time and again.

At my urging, the two groups discussed this issue and the project managers were chagrined and surprised to learn how much business savvy the architects really had—but from a totally different perspective. The architects were striving for a previously unspoken goal—the thrill of having their work featured in an architectural journal. The project managers learned that the most common criteria for this honor was—innovation! The architects weren't creating original designs to be annoying. Within the industry paradigm, innovation was a legitimate way of contributing to the prestige and reputation of the company and attracting affluent clients to the firm.

Once the project managers understood this, their irritability and judgment of the architects was replaced with professional respect. Their new attitudes were clearly communicated to the architects, which ended the power struggles and gamesmanship. The quality of their collaborations skyrocketed.

A Cycle of Contempt:
The crew chiefs and their new hires

This next cycle illustrates how accurately others mirror our behaviors. I was invited to work at a company with extremely harsh working conditions. The men who worked on these crews repaired endless miles of railroad tracks and performed taxing manual labor in harsh weather conditions. The crews traveled continuously, moving along the track and changing hotel rooms every other night. They took their days off alone. Without access to a vehicle, they spent their downtime in a barren motel room watching TV.

Every three months they went home for two weeks. Their hourly pay was lower than they would have made at a fast-food restaurant. Only substantial amounts of overtime made their work financially rewarding.

However, when their human resource director, Sam, began an initiative to decrease the company's high turnover, he didn't focus on reducing the physical demands of their work, and improving their pay or working conditions. Instead he focused on the crew chiefs' ability to motivate and manage their teams.

During exit interviews Sam had learned that employees weren't quitting because of time away from home, low hourly pay, or physical hardship. The most frequently cited reason for leaving was the disrespectful tone of the crew chiefs. When Sam told me this I was reminded of an old saying: "People will forget what you did, and they will forget what you said, but they will never forget how you made them feel."

Sam had heard about my seminars and asked me to work with the chiefs to improve their ability to manage teams in taxing, isolated settings.

During the seminar, one of the crew chiefs focused on a frustration that every one of the supervisors faced—a newly hired employee whose performance was below standards.

Addressing the problem of an underperforming employee, the crew chief responded to **#1** ("Frustration") "A new operator is not pulling his weight."

Responding to **#2** with negative, reflexive thinking, the crew chief assumed the employee's poor performance was due to his personality and wrote, "The new hire is lazy."

The crew chief wrote after **#3** (My behavior): "Embarrass him in front of the other guys. Point out his mistakes and make him an example."

When the crew chief moved underneath the line on the Cycle of Contempt, he had to put himself in the shoes of the new hire and look at his own behavior through his employee's eyes (**#4**). He realized that from the employee's perspective, the new operator would see: "My boss ridicules me to get a laugh." What's the negative conclusion (**#5**) the operator would make about his chief? "He treats me like an idiot and he sets me up. My boss is a jerk. In fact, the whole company stinks."

If the operator floods with the chemicals associated with hostility, learning new skills will be more difficult and his errors will increase. (Remember John Gottman's discovery in his biofeedback work? If someone floods and their heartbeat goes above 100 beats per minute, he or she can't hear. *Even if they try.*)

When the chief responded to **#6** (The operator's behavior), he realized that the new hire would "Find other guys who hate the boss and make his life living hell." When the chief moved above the horizontal line back into his world he wrote after **#7** ("what I see or hear"), "The new hire is a loser and troublemaker." This is negative reciprocity in the raw, and this reality wasn't lost on the chief. As he completed the last steps he was confronted with the self-defeating nature of his own behavior.

During the seminar, all the crew chiefs and supervisors had hung their Cycles of Contempt on the wall for the other participants to read.

After the crew chief finished his cycle, the entire class gathered in front of it in dead silence. No one dismissed what he had drawn. They realized their colleague was dead-on accurate.

For the first time, the chiefs realized how critical their attitudes were in setting the tone for their men. In their situation, with exhausting work, low pay, extreme isolation, and confined working conditions, the energy of contempt destroyed the team *and* made their jobs as supervisors more stressful and difficult.

A Cycle of Courage:
The crew chiefs and their new hires

When the supervisor analyzed the problem of new hires using a more reflective orientation, he realized he was dealing with a systems problem. The applicants who responded to the company's recruitment efforts had much less skill and experience than entry-level workers in the past.

Fifteen years ago, most of their new hires were graduates of technical schools. They could read schematics and understood the fundamentals of electricity, welding, and so on. However, most of their current employees weren't technical school graduates; the majority were high school dropouts.

During our discussions the crew chiefs acknowledged the declining levels of training in their hiring pool. The conversation turned to the fact that the company hadn't changed its training program to adjust to this shift. The real problem wasn't the personalities or motivation of the new hires. The problem originated in the fact that most of their applicants needed more extensive, and basic, training than their current orientation provided. Despite the growing knowledge gap between the job requirements and the skills of their recruits, the company had been running the same training program for more than 15 years.

When the crew chief drew his second cycle, the Cycle of Courage, his attitude toward the operators changed dramatically.

From that point onward, when a new hire began to flounder, the chiefs were more likely to be analytical, and far less inflammatory, about the problem. The chiefs realized that to do otherwise was self-defeating.

Of course, not all operators were able to meet minimum performance standards. Some weren't willing or able to perform the work the company required, and crew chiefs had to terminate them. However, using warmth and encouragement rather than contempt, they were more successful in retaining the employees who had the capacity to learn the skills the job required, and the seasoned veterans were relieved when the hostility and negativity of their work situation lightened. For the first time, crews had an opportunity to become real teams.

In follow-up conversations Sam, the human resource director, told me that the chiefs had become more patient and encouraging—attributes of great supervisors.

A Cycle of Contempt:
The alienated son

Dennis, a participant in a public works seminar, is the basis of the next example. Dennis was gifted and secure in the world of machines, but had less confidence in his ability to parent. However, he carried his two teenage sons close to his heart.

During the seminar, when Dennis was asked to identify something in his life that troubled him, he sat quietly for a long time. Finally, he acknowledged that his relationship with his 16 year-old son, Aaron, was on rocky ground. Dennis was the father of two boys and when his older son, Jade, had turned 16, he had become sullen and withdrawn. Now Aaron, his younger child, had reached this critical age and Dennis feared that he too would retreat.

The first step in drawing the cycles is stating the facts. Responding to question **#1**. ("Frustration) on his Cycle of Contempt Dennis wrote, "Aaron has just turned 16, and he's withdrawn."

Dennis's thinking about Aaron's watershed year was fairly pessimistic, so after **#2** he wrote what he had been thinking for some time: "It's impossible to communicate with Aaron now that he's a teenager. It's useless to try."

During class, Dennis and I worked together to identify how this thinking affected his behavior. Dennis realized that because he assumed Aaron would withdraw, *he* had started to withdraw from Aaron. He continued to do things with his older son, but because he expected to be turned down by Aaron, he wrote after **#3** ("My behavior"): "Make plans with his brother, Jade."

When Dennis moved to **#4** ("What they see or hear"), he put himself in Aaron's shoes. What did Aaron notice about Dad's subtle withdrawal? Imagine you're a 16-year-old male. Your father, who's been the center of your life, continues to hunt and go ice fishing with your older brother, but without including you in the plans. Dad extends an invitation to you, but it seems half-hearted, and comes after the dates and details have already been set.

Through Aaron's eyes Dad's behavior might look like, "Dad seeks out my older brother more. They do things together." When Dad had to guess at **#5** (Aaron's negative conclusion), he surprised himself by writing: "Jade is Dad's favorite."

If this conclusion is Aaron's understandable assumption, he would most likely protect himself from feelings of rejection by withdrawing— exactly what Dennis was seeing.

Dennis told me that the amount of time Aaron spent at home was plummeting. After **#6** he wrote from Aaron's perspective, "Forget both of them! I'll hang out with my girlfriend or buddies."

Before Dennis drew his cycle, he hadn't considered the possibility that Aaron's behavior was a reaction to his own. When Dennis saw his son withdrawing, it confirmed his belief. "See! 16 year-olds are impossible."

Without a change in awareness, father and son might go around this cycle once, or hundreds of times, reacting to each other's behavior. And feelings of hurt and rejection would likely follow.

I told Dennis's story in a subsequent seminar and a participant, Wendy, came up on break to tell me about a similar and particularly painful cycle from her life. Years ago her younger brother, Ray, had become addicted to cocaine. At the height of his addiction he stole his mother's car. In a desperate attempt to stop his decline, their mother called the police. Ray was arrested and this incident, combined with several others, led to his serving time in prison.

During his imprisonment Ray and his mother had no communication. However, after his release Wendy forced a meeting between the two. During the initially awkward meeting they discovered that each of them had been pining for a reunion, but assumed the other person was bitter and angry, and would rebuke the invitation. Because he had stolen her car, Ray assumed his mother did not want to see him again. His mother was shocked when she heard this. *She* had assumed Ray would refuse contact with her because she had reported him to the police!

Both had spent several years longing for a connection and feeling rejected. Neither person had the skill or courage to reach out. Not until Wendy forced a reunion did they discover their mistake.

Early in my career I expected to find malice at the root of most conflicts. However, I learned that it is much more common to find *hurt*, based on real or perceived rejection. In our culture it is not easy for people to admit they feel excluded or disrespected, especially in work settings. Consequently, many individuals express their sense of loss through anger and withdrawal. The desire to be connected and respected is ancient and intrinsic, and people generally give up only after they conclude it's useless to try. However, when conditions change most people are remarkably forgiving. The desire to belong overrides their hurt.

I've had many clients draw and share Cycles of Contempt on longstanding divisions within their families. It is truly painful to see their work. Everyone in class is moved. People everywhere are mourning separation from children, siblings, partners, former best friends, parents, and in-laws. Often, when they do this exercise they realize, as I did with Alicia's father (in the story depicted in the appendix), that not only is *their* behavior fueling the problem, they hold the power to break the cycle.

A Cycle of Courage:
The alienated son

After a break, Dennis returned, his seat and drew a Cycle of Courage to address his relationship with Aaron. He didn't change the facts or his response to question #1. Aaron was still 16 and still withdrawn.

However, on step **#2**, Dennis changed his thinking. Instead of inflammatory, personality-based thinking, Dennis responded to **#2** by writing, "He's busy and his peers are more important."

In response to question **#3**, Dennis wrote, "I'll work around Aaron's schedule and plan activities that include his friends."

This new behavior requires patience and confidence. To act on this new approach Dennis would have to risk being rejected by Aaron. Hence Cycles of Courage call for just that—courage.

Although we don't know for certain that Aaron would respond in the above manner, one thing is obvious: Dennis is making it perfectly clear to Aaron how important his son is to him. He's eliminated the possibility that Aaron will misunderstand his behavior, priorities, and availability, and Dennis might avoid the unnecessary alienation experienced by the mother and her incarcerated son.

A Cycle of Contempt:
The angry police chief and the press

I think the last cycle shows more than any why I named positive reciprocity "Cycles of *Courage*." However, the following also serves to emphasize the connection.

After a sexual assault occurred in a small town, the editor of the local paper published facts about the case that the police chief wanted withheld. The chief's reflexive response was to blame the editor.

When he used the Cycle of Contempt to diagram his reactions, he put the facts after **#1**: "The editor reported on an assault case in a way that compromised the investigation." For question **#2** the chief wrote his contemptuous thinking: "All the editor cares about is selling newspapers, like all people in the media!" Under **#3** he wrote how he would behave if he acted on this thinking: "Restrict the editor's access to additional information."

However, when the chief moved onto question **#4**, he had to put himself in the editor's shoes. He realized that the editor would observe that the chief was withholding public information. For question **#5** ("imagine *you* are the editor") the chief considered how the editor would interpret that this fact. The chief realized the editor might conclude the police had something to hide or were restricting access because of complicity in the crime.

In question **#6** the chief was asked to imagine how the editor would likely respond to a potential cover up where the police department had wrongly concealed information vital to the public good? It's likely, the chief reasoned, that the editor would feel indignant and retaliate. He might blast the chief in the newspaper, hire an investigator to find his own evidence, or use the courts to force the release of information.

For question **#7** the chief used his conclusion from the previous response—the editor had gone on the attack and is working around the chief and against him—to confirm his negative assumption about the editor: "All he cares about is selling papers. See, I was right." Like the story of Aaron and his father, the chief and the editor could remain in a Cycle of Contempt for days, months, or the rest of their working relationship.

A Cycle of Courage:
The angry police chief and the press

After we talked about the problem-solving orientation, the chief returned to his situation. The frustrating event was the same: "The editor damaged the investigation." However, responding to question **#2** the chief made the assumption that the editor was reasonable, and the problem was rooted in something else. He wrote, "He's probably an okay guy. However, he might not know a lot about police investigations." This is a more reflective, and probably a more accurate analysis of the problem than his previous assumptions.

Now, when the chief thinks about the editor's behavior the chief is inclined to visit him and explain how his article impaired the case. If the editor sees that the chief is frustrated, but reasonable and conciliatory, what might the editor conclude about the chief? He might think that "The chief is a straight-shooter. He wants this crime solved and the article we ran hampered his work." By changing his thinking, the chief would be able to change the direction of their relationship.

The chief told me that he had overcome his initial, reflexive response. He *did* go visit the editor, and the editor responded with gratitude. As their conversation drew to a close the editor said to him, "I've seen a lot of chiefs come and go in this town. This is the first time one of them has had the guts to tell me to me to my face that he was unhappy about something I did. I appreciate it. That took a lot of guts." The chief had laid the foundation for a solid working relationship.

Cycles of Contempt on large scales

Cycles of Contempt can occur between two people, or two million. Once you understand how they work, you will see them everywhere. They happen in corporations, government, nonprofits, families, neighborhoods, gangs, faith communities, and nations.

Several years ago there was a shooting at the high school from which I graduated. At the time, reporters interviewed the students and asked them, "Why do you bring guns to school?" The answer, across the board, was, "Because other students are carrying them."

If I were currently a student, I might carry a weapon for self-protection, but other students might not know my reasoning. They would perceive that I am carrying a weapon in order to harm them. How would they response to their observation? By arming themselves! What do I see? They're bringing weapons to school! It validates my fear that I am at risk and need to be prepared to protect myself.

Cycles of Contempt also apply to conflict between nations. Each nation perceives the buildup of arms by a neighboring country as possible aggression, but views their own armament as self-protection—similar to the escalation of nuclear arms by Pakistan and India. Reciprocity is a common theme throughout history.

International mediators have prevented the escalation of aggressive behavior by asking heads of state, "If you build up your stockpile of arms, how will your neighbors perceive your actions? And what will they do in return?"

This important insight isn't used often in the workplace. When you are frustrated, a reflexive, inflammatory response might prompt you to attack the other person's reputation or withdraw. However, before you *act*, ask, "How will the other party view my behavior?"

Many clients have told me they use the question "How will my actions be perceived?" on a regular basis. You may be surprised how often you change your behavior in reaction to the answer. By tracking the likely reaction to your behavior, you will be consciously shaping your world and the quality of relationships.

You *are* the center of *your* universe

The tone and intention of your messages and behaviors are returned to you with very reliable predictability. Hostility toward others is self-defeating. Using less inflammatory thinking increases your chances of a good outcome, as these cycles clearly demonstrate. From here forward you can observe these principles and use them to your benefit.

In the next chapter we'll take these concepts even further and you'll learn more strategies for turning Cycles of Contempt into Cycles of Courage.

Chapter Eight

Hard on the Problem,
Soft on the People:
The True Causes of Workplace
Conflict and Stress

The line between good and evil lies in the center of every human heart.

—Alexander Solzhenitsyn

Myron Tribus, one of the grandfathers of lean manufacturing and process improvement said, "The job of management is to remove barriers to pride in work."

In the *reflective* thinking pattern one assumes that people *want* to be part of a functioning, healthy work group, and have an intrinsic desire for achieving reasonable goals and meeting the expectations of their customers and supervisors.

Although this innate drive can be, and often is, extinguished by poorly designed systems and climates of hostility and disrespect, it can also be reactivated when conditions improve. Approaching problems with this assumption is critical to your effectiveness.

Whenever tension is high or morale is languishing, assume that *something*—a policy, workflow, anxiety, fear, miscommunication, negative reciprocity—is blocking the person's or group's ability to achieve, become part of a team, and feel valued. It's rare that this assumption is not accurate.

People have strong needs for a sense of belonging. When workplaces don't provide an opportunity for respect, camaraderie, and attachment, individuals make their emotional investments in unions, local bars, gangs, recreational activities, home-based businesses, faith communities, or families.

A manager of a customer service department told me, as a means of introduction to his direct reports, that they "only worked for the paycheck." He viewed his 18 employees as working mothers who had taken jobs only to provide a second income to their families. Consequently, the manager made no investment in their development nor did he solicit their ideas for improving customer service. When I interviewed his direct reports, I checked his assumption and found that almost 50 percent of his group had part-time, home-based businesses, from craft shows to catering. He was right—they weren't making an investment in work, but only because he had denied them the opportunities and experiences that allow those desires to develop.

Human nature is vulnerable to the system

People behave differently depending on constraints, pressures, peer pressure, anxiety levels, time urgency, and so on. This notion is fairly well-accepted in academic circles, but is not widely recognized by business leaders. Most individuals think about people as either good or bad, lazy or ambitious. In reality, people aren't that static or one-dimensional. Every human being has a range of behaviors from which they choose. Even people who are deemed unsalvageable by the courts have the capacity to surprise. Felons with no hope for parole volunteer to raise seeing-eye dogs, or provide hospice care to aging inmates. Even Larry Trapp, the Grand Dragon of the Klu Klux Klan from Chapter Two, who most people would dismiss as hopeless, was capable of changing.

The other side of human nature is also true. "Ordinary" people are capable of malfeasance when trapped in corrupt systems.

Changing systems changes behavior

Personality is malleable. In the book *The Cheating Culture,* author David Callahan documents the decline of formerly trustworthy Sears auto mechanics in 1990s, when their compensation system underwent a dramatic change. Corporate decision-makers lowered the base pay of both managers and mechanics. Suddenly, workers were forced to compensate for their drop in income (and perhaps increase it dramatically) by selling parts and additional services. The mechanics and their managers were driven into the harsh position of having to choose between ethics and economic security.

Within a few years, Sears's sterling customer service ratings plummeted, and 18 class-action suits and scores of investigations for fraudulent practices were brought against the company.

This is an important insight for organizations. Workplaces are constantly required to challenge, motivate, and mediate human behavior. At one level this insight means that, by changing structure, rewards, and performance criteria, organizations can change behavior. Or looking through the other side of the lens: if management isn't satisfied with current behavior, they can go upstream and change the conditions that are causing undesired outcomes.

Philip Zimbardo, from Stanford University, explored a much darker side of how situations shape behavior. His findings, published in *Obedience to Authority: Current Perspectives on the Milgram Paradigm* (1999), eerily foreshadowed criminal behavior at Abu Ghraib prison during the Iraq War.

In the 1980s, Zimbardo turned the bottom floor of the University of California psychology building into a simulated "prison," complete with iron bars and a solitary confinement cell. Zimbardo and his associates tested, interviewed, and identified 24 psychologically healthy college students to tak part in the experiement, and divided them into two groups consisting of "prisoners" and "guards." The original plan was to run the experiment for two weeks.

However, on the sixth day of the mock prison experiment, Christine Maslach, a friend and colleague who hadn't previously been involved in the project, stopped in to assist with interviews. Christine described what she saw with dismay, "I looked at the line of hooded, shuffling, chained prisoners, with guards shouting orders at them—and then quickly averted my gaze. I was overwhelmed by a chilling, sickening feeling." Zimbardo wrote, "We observed and documented that the guards steadily increased their coercive and aggressive tactics, humiliation, and dehumanization of the prisoners day by day."

Maslach confronted Zimbardo with his complicity in a college psychology experiment that had dangerously deteriorated and needed to be terminated. At first Zimbardo disagreed with her. However, to his credit, he eventually acknowledged that Christine's observations were accurate and ended the experiment. Later he wrote that his role as the chief researcher had been compromised by his role as a prison superintendent who had been eager "to maintain the integrity of *my prison*" (italics added).

Situations have a huge effect on human behavior. Competitive systems with harsh economic norms result in aggressive, and sometimes unethical, behavior. In contrast, systems that are seen as accessible, fair, rewarding, and cooperative bring out the best in people. In the book *No Contest*, Alfie Kohn documents this finding in detail.

Elliot Aronson of Stanford University also conducted experiments loaded with insight for workplaces. Aronson, a specialist in school shooting rampages, cites a study from the Secret Service. Analysing 41 student shooting rampage perpetrators, the Secret Service found no way to distinguish perpetrators from others based on their "personality, attitudes or demographics." Aronson turned his attention to the context in which this act occurs. His conclusions are chilling. "The root cause of the shootings is the poisonous social atmosphere that exists in almost every public school in this country—atmospheres permeated by daily incidents of exclusion, taunting, bullying, and humiliation." A comment from a Columbine football player after the shootings serves as a vivid example: "Columbine is a good, clean place except for those rejects."

Of particular value to our purpose is Aronson's ability to improve relationships between elementary students by simply changing the system in which the students learn. Aronson coached teachers to shift from a competitive to cooperative learning format, where student's work was interdependent rather than competitive. Within two weeks, group-mates have gone from taunting, to encouraging each other. Lasting friendships were formed across cultural and language differences—differences that had been the basis of exclusion and taunting just days prior to the change.

This is another example of the difference between focusing on people (in our paradigm BO and BS) as the source of problems and focusing on the situation or system (BIBS).

Throughout history, the really fundamental changes in societies have come about not from dictates of governments and the results of battles but through vast numbers of people changing their minds—sometimes only a little bit...By deliberately changing the internal image of reality, people can change the world. Perhaps the only limits to the human mind are those we believe in.

—Willis Harman,
Global Mind Change

In escalated conflict it's difficult to assess the potential performance of any employee. During power struggles, *everyone's* "evil twin" emerges. If management is unclear about an employee's capacities during escalated conflict, I suggest that we reduce barriers to pride in work, eliminate system inefficiencies and waste, lower fear, and end power struggles. Then wait a reasonable period of time to assess performance. If, under ideal conditions, employees cannot meet realistic performance standards, management must proceed with consequences including, if necessary, termination.

With that disclaimer in place, let's look at some of the situations when reasonable people behave poorly at work.

First: Is there a baby in the back seat?

Always assume that the other party has multiple hidden constraints or pressures that are shaping his or her behavior. For a quick review of high conflict situations where one or both parties ignored this step, see Chapter Four. Of course, this assumption may be wrong, and there is no pressing reality of which you are unaware. But it doesn't take much time to sit down with someone and ask for help in understanding his or her behavior.

When I've taken this step, I haven't always discovered a hidden reason. Sometimes it takes time to build trust, or there is fear of punishment, or organizational retribution is too high. There are cases where clients *are* hiding illegal or unethical behaviors. However, I've *never* regretted asking. In the next chapter you'll learn a simple technique for opening the dialogue and clarifying whether or not people are blocked by hidden contingencies.

Second: Look at your systems and processes

There are many books and courses on system thinking and process mapping. These techniques are taught at universities, nonprofit organizations, and consulting firms. The information falls under different names and formats such as Total Quality, the Baldridge Award, Lean, manufacturing, and process improvement. Many organizations have gained tremendous improvements by learning how to remove waste from their processes and streamlining workflow.

In conflict resolution work I sometimes teach my clients an introduction to process-mapping in one day. My comments here will be limited to

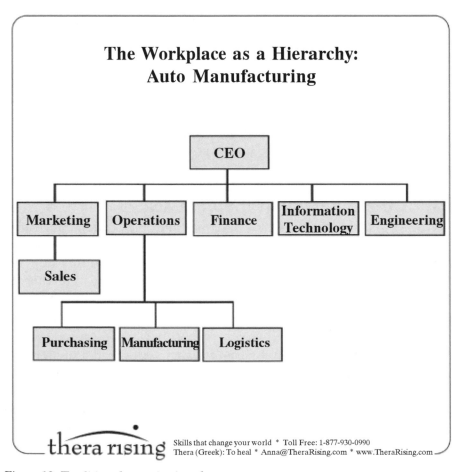

Figure 12. Traditional organization chart

how you can use this perspective to eliminate the true sources of stress and conflict.

During the industrial revolution, organizational charts of the workplace were based on military models of command and control (figure 12). It's no wonder—most of the men who built the first industrial workplaces were former officers during the Civil War. Traditional organizational charts delineate authority and responsibility, but they do not portray the interdependency of departments, or the flow of work through an organization.

In contrast, *system perspectives* (Figure 13) track workflow from the beginning of the organization's processes to the end. It's multifunctional, fluid, and loops back on itself.

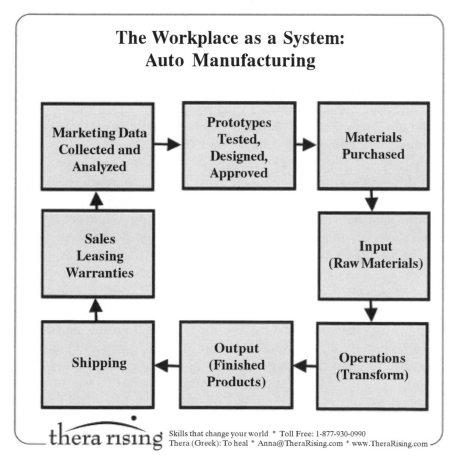

Figure 13. The workplace as a system

A very simplified systems perspective of an automobile manufacturer might begin with market research determining the next sought-after features or vehicles; engineering completing feasibility studies, prototypes, and final designs; purchasing translating production goals into the necessary raw materials (circuit boards, steel, fiberglass, wiring) for operations, orders, and purchases; production taking raw materials and transforming them into outputs (finished cars); shipping providing transportation to dealers; distributors overseeing leases and sales; service and sales tracking warranty, safety, and service data; cross-functional teams studying after-sales information to feed back into their system. Then the whole cycle starts anew by the organization gearing up for the new generation of production.

What I just described is a very, very complex, interconnected system. How well do most systems work? It depends. How savvy are the leaders about systems thinking? When problems occur, do individuals from other departments join together to solve them, or do they break into Cycles of Contempt? Do employees understand the delicate interdependence of their work and take other departments into consideration as they make decisions? For instance, does engineering invite shipping to their planning meetings to discuss changes in product dimensions and how those changes will impact the number of vehicles that can be transported by rail or container vessel?

Most workplace systems contain *2,000* or more processes. Each process requires that someone take what's given to him or her (input) and transform and deliver a product or service (output). Output can be a design, a toaster, an ice-cream cone, a budget, an e-mail system, a document, or an after-school program. Service industries, schools, government bodies—any organization can draw their work as a system or series of linking processes.

When I'm doing team building or conflict resolution, I often create a simple process map with clients. Working in small groups and hanging our work on the wall, we use Post-it notes for each step and place them on big sheets of flip chart paper. Post-it notes are great because they're flexible. They can be lifted and repositioned as many times as necessary. We create the process as it should be, and then how it really works. Lightbulbs flash when people see how much of their conflict is related to dysfunctional processes, not people.

For example, imagine a process improvement team wants to focus on improving the existing process for qualifying a new customer for credit. They would start by identifying the steps it takes to accomplish this task. Do they collect information from the customer? If yes, that's the first step of the process. Do they verify the information? That's the second step of the process, and so on. In process improvement we ask questions such as: What's the sequence of the steps? Who's involved? Where are decisions made that require a branch in the flow chart based on the outcome of the decision?

After we reach consensus about workplace flow, we look for sources of waste, delays, or unnecessary steps. The team might look for bottlenecks: does the application sits on someone's desk for days or weeks? Is everyone doing the work the same way, or are there variations, rework, and confusion? How many delays, bottlenecks, shortages, or overruns can the team reduce or eliminate?

In most organizations, what percentage of the 2,000 processes would you guess are poorly designed or inefficient? Almost *all* of them!

Most workplace processes were never consciously designed, they just evolved. As a result, they are full of idiosyncrasies, poorly defined steps, or unnecessary tasks. For instance, a process improvement team at a manufacturing site questioned why the shipping department put a piece of cardboard on top of their products before they sealed the box. *No one knew.* The mystery wasn't solved until a team member tracked down a retired employee who said, "Well, son, we started that practice in 1942 as a means of keeping the product clean, because at that time we sealed the boxes with a glue brush." They had continued the practice for decades past its usefulness.

Imagine the improvements in efficiency and morale if organizations could improve key processes by even 5 percent! Dr. Deming, one of the most effective workplace change agents of all times, believed that 85 to 93 percent of workplace waste originates in *systems,* not *people*. He became famous for witty harangues of managers who had hounded employees to improve productivity when, in reality, most *employees* had zero authority to change systems and processes of their workflow. His colleague, Myron Tribus said, "Employees work in a system. It's the job of management to work on the system and improve it, continuously, with their help."

Whenever I enter a high-conflict situation, I always start with the assumption that the conflict's root causes are in the systems, and act accordingly. The odds are in my favor. In resolving more than 120 conflicts, only twice have I found the root cause of the problem was a key person who lacked the capacity to do his or her job.

In *every* other situation I've stepped into, conflict escalated precisely because everyone involved had taken the position of "This is a mess, whose fault is it?" By starting with this question, the true causes of tension had been overlooked.

If you start with the assumption that people are reasonable and a constraint or pressure in the system is fueling tension and negative behavior, you'll not only eliminate most of the systemic reasons for stress and blame at work, you'll become remarkably efficient in solving your organization's problems.

When problems and disagreements occur or chronic tension exists between two groups, is something in the system out of whack? Are systems bogged down with rework, bottlenecks, or ambiguity? Do differences in performance measures between one group and another put people at odds? Is there a more efficient way to do this job? What causes confusion and resentment?

The following is another story about millions of dollars that were lost because individuals locked horns in a power struggle over personalities, rather than joining together to solve a catastrophic systems problem.

The genius that dissed the president

Rick, a technical genius, had narrowly escaped being fired after he "lipped off" to the company president. Most of the executive team viewed Rick as an unprofessional, undisciplined hothead who enjoyed exploiting the fact that he was central to one of their most important processes: customized machines.

One thing was clear; Rick's job was critical. If a salesperson wanted a machine customized (the majority of the company's sales), Rick was the man they had to deal with—but Rick's average time for turning around an estimate for a customization request was three months! The sales people were livid—they told me they were losing 25 percent of their sales and millions of dollars to this delay.

The situation between Rick and the sales group had deteriorated so badly that during the annual sales meeting, Virg, the vice president of the division, told his sales team, "Rick is the organization's number-one barrier to sales."

The company president told me that Rick would have been terminated months ago if anyone else in the company came close to matching his capabilities. The president gave me carte blanche to do what I needed in order to fix *him*.

By the time I was done collecting background information, I half-expected Rick to be a surly, arrogant, sociopath. Instead, I found someone who cared so much about his work that he talked for four hours about his frustrations, resentments, multiple attempts to resolve his huge backlog, how hard he had tried to become more effective, and how stymied he felt in his attempts to obtain the resources and cooperation he needed to do his job.

Rick also told me that after he heard about Virg's negative comment at the sales meeting, he lost all motivation to overcome the backlog, had quit working overtime, and had fallen further behind—a perfect example of negative reciprocity.

As Rick's story wound down, I made it very, very clear that we were about to turn in his resignation as the company scapegoat, and take unprecedented steps to fix the problem at it's true source. The company had a lousy process for securing quotes, and Rick couldn't fix the process by himself.

During my initial conversations with Rick, I consciously used the power of appreciation and its ability to bond. It's the fastest way to gain commitment to a hardheaded search for solutions. When Rick wrapped up his story, he knew I had truly listened and acknowledged the validity of his frustrations, respected his dedication, and been impressed by the many creative ways he had tried to resolve the backlog. He felt validated and appreciated.

Not until this point could I be successful in giving him the critical feedback *he* needed to hear. With a grin, I told him that although the organization could take the lion's share of responsibility for the bottleneck, his defensiveness and "complete lack of social skills" with the president didn't help.

I delivered my comments with warmth. The relationship we forged during our first meeting allowed me to speak to Rick bluntly. Even though I had only known him for four hours, Rick laughed good-naturedly at my frank, but accurate, remarks. He knew he had to alter his approach to achieve the changes he so desperately needed.

Rick lacked the skill and positional power to address a problem that deeply affected his reputation and relationships. The process needing repair spanned three divisions, and required the involvement of management four levels above him. Because Rick *couldn't* fix the problem, his relationships with the sales group became more adversarial. He'd become bitter, sullen, "unprofessional," and "undisciplined."

Within a few days of our first meeting, Rick and I sat down with the vice presidents of engineering and sales. I asked Rick to share his perceptions of the root causes of his current backlog, and, as a group, using the PostIt and flip-chart paper method, we flow-charted the current process for procuring an estimate on a customized machine.

The VP of engineering was shocked to learn that when Rick approached an engineer for (yet another) quote, they ducked into offices to avoid him. As a result, every piece of information Rick needed to formulate his quotes entailed a laborious, time-consuming process of multiple, unreturned e-mails and phone calls.

Rick and Virg, the VP of sales, had their first ever prolonged, face-to-face conversation. Virg learned that the salespeople (with Virg's encouragement) had been loading their requests for estimates with every conceivable feature, knowing full well the customer would never pay the premium dollars it took to build them.

However, customizations were the company's market niche, and complex orders were one of the ways the sales group played up the organization's capacities. Unfortunately, each one of these features complicated and delayed Rick's work. When Rick tried to tell the salespeople that the extraneous features were making the problem worse, they dismissed him as a blowhard; especially, Rick continued, after their vice president had christened him "the number-one barrier to sales."

Virg dropped his eyes when he realized that one of his salespeople had told Rick about the denigrating remark. Then Virg spontaneously—and with genuine remorse—apologized for the callous remark. A flash of relief crossed Rick's face.

The four of us turned our attention to the wasteful and haphazard process. During the next hour and a half we generated several significant changes for streamlining it and clearing up Rick's backlog. The next morning the two VPs met with their teams and announced the changes. Rick began a daily 8 a.m. staff meeting with a cross-functional team consisting of engineering, software, and sales. The meetings averaged an hour. With everyone in the room to review requests and rough out estimates, the process went from days to minutes.

The VP of engineering designed a rotating roster that assured at least two of his engineers and a software designer would be available at the start of each day. Virg appointed a gatekeeper within sales. All requests for customized machines had to pass muster for extraneous features before they left the sales group and reached Rick's desk. Over the next few months Rick's backlog dropped from three months to a few days. The sales team was ecstatic. This gave them a tremendous competitive edge.

Six months later, Rick was an honored guest at the annual sales meeting. He took the podium to talk about the next generation of possibilities in customized designs. The president of the company later told me that he estimated they saved $1.5 million in sales the first year after the changes were implemented.

This story is a perfect example of the cost savings that can be realized by shifting from reflexive, inflammatory thinking (BO) to searching for the *reasons* (BIBS) in processes and systems that drive people's behavior.

Menopause Molly

In another situation, a vice president, desperate to resolve a widespread problem in his service department, told me privately that I needed to come in and "fix Molly," the service technician coordinator. Molly, he confided, was going home early twice a week in tears. "Problems with menopause," he whispered.

When the leadership team and I shifted the focus from her "unreasonable *personality*" onto their poorly designed *systems*, the cost savings her department accrued ran into the millions. It was another situation where the people who were suffering the most also were the biggest contributors to the problem. Once we gathered a cross-functional team of decision-makers, the process problem was embarrassingly easy to fix.

The current generation of workers and senior executives will probably be the last to have finished formal education *without* systems thinking. If your company isn't learning process mapping or systems thinking, I would highly encourage you to search out a competent training program and add those techniques to your skills-set. Once employees and leaders begin to view work through a systems perspective, interconnectedness of efforts is highlighted, and they *self-correct* behavior that causes problems down-stream.

Third: Look for conflicting performance measures

Pay attention to the type of behavior your systems feed. Avoid performance measures and bonuses that emphasize competition and pit individuals against each other.

I have more than once found that the root cause of conflict between executives is often embedded in the criteria upon which their bonuses are calculated. Each person is working specific criteria to maximize their bonus, but at the expense of cross-functional collaboration.

Often, by working with a company's CFO and CEO, we've changed team dynamics from adversarial to cooperative by backing away from individual performance measures based on departmental accomplishments, to basing everyone's bonus on the same measure—such as year-end profitability.

In one setting, within 24 hours of the change, the VP of sales offered the VP of operations—his previous scapegoat—an unfilled employee position to help allieviate his staff shortage. Why did the formerly self-oriented executive suddenly become so cooperative? Because we made it in his best interest to help his colleagues succeed! These results are similar to what Aronson experienced when he changed the system of learning in schools.

If bonuses, systems, award programs, and performance measures encourage cooperation and interdependence, then those type of behavior are amplified. In Chapter Eleven we'll look at strategies that maintain cultures of cooperation and respect.

Fourth: Many inappropriate behaviors are the result of low skill, insight, or courage

First, let's unravel blaming, inflammatory thinking. It's a thinking pattern that assumes there's no possible way to reason with another person or group—they are flawed beyond hope, and therefore our aggressive and exclusionary behaviors are justified. Before we focus further on this thinking pattern I need to tell you a story about blame's stinky twin—depression.

In 1978 a team of psychologists (Abramson, Seligman, and Teasdal) specializing in cognitive therapy—the study of thinking patterns, or self-talk—were contacted by a company that had terminated a significant number of employees. Most of the former employees began a job search in a relatively short period of time, and took full advantage of outplacement resources.

However, a small group of former workers had become depressed and were managing their job search half-heartedly, or not at all. The company asked the therapists to help. Because the psychologists specialized in cognitive therapy, they assumed the reason the sub-group became lethargic was because of what they were saying to themselves about the cause of their terminations.

The findings of these practitioners changed the field of psychology. Through interviews with depressed former employees, the psychologists identified the concepts of *personal*, *pervasive*, and *permanent*. First, the depressed, unemployed workers concluded that their loss of employment was *personal*, despite the fact that many people lost their jobs. The depressed, passive group attributed their loss solely to their own behavior. They used self-talk statements such as, "This was my fault. I should have worked more overtime," or, "I should have seen this coming and left that sinking ship a year ago." The tendency to blame a misfortune solely on one's personal behavior is called personalization—the assumption that a negative outcome is totally the fault of the individual.

The second thinking pattern psychologist identified was a tendency to make self-criticisms *pervasive*. They judged every element of their lives in a negative light. "Not only can't I hold down a job, I'm a bad parent, and my garden is dead. I'm a complete failure."

They magnified their feelings of unworthiness by telling themselves that their job-loss was *permanent*. "Never again will I have interesting work." (As the comedian Robin Williams quips, "Whenever I start feeling unmotivated to look for work there's always one thought that immediately shifts my mood, 'Want fries with that?'")

These three conclusions—personal, pervasive, and permanent—are deadly in combination. When people fall into this trap they are overwhelmed by a sense of hopelessness and failure.

These statements are also the thinking patterns of blame. The only difference is the direction of the arrow. *In depression, the arrow of contempt points inward. In blame, contempt points toward another person or group.* Anger, irritability, and the automatic assumption that *someone* is to blame, become invisible habits that sap people's energy, relationships, effectiveness, health, and vitality. A downward spiral ensues.

Depression, or self-loathing, is a worse state than hostility. It feels awful *and* it lacks energy. While hostility is emotionally stressful, it has an advantage over depression in that it carries a jolt of energy. At work, people often use the energy of hostility to escape the numbness of depression. One of the most common ways to escape debilitating depression is by turning contempt toward an external target, activating adrenaline, and pumping up feelings of superiority. The same thinking pattern results in both hostility and depression, depending on which way the pointing finger swings. Neither one of them solves problems. As a result, problems accumulate and intensify. Life becomes more unmanageable and lonely. When you react to frustration with blame, either toward yourself or others, you set up a reoccurring dynamic between depression and hostility.

Now we can see exactly why hostility and depression are linked. The thinking patterns are identical; they have the same DNA; it's all your (my) fault, it's everything about you (me), you (I) can't change.

An effective attitude for addressing problems

So, what's the alternative? How does one think about others' destructive or inappropriate behavior in a more useful way? Destructive behavior on the part of other people is not going away, and there's plenty of it.

Again, in order to be more effective you don't have to take a "Pollyanna" approach, covering your eyes to block out reality, and think, "Isn't everyone WONDERFUL!?" In fact, the opposite approach is more useful. *Assume everyone, including you, is a nutcase.* Everyone is flawed. So what's to be gained by getting indignant and flooding?

Every day, each of us hits a "growing edge" where we don't have what it takes to do the correct thing or make the right decision. Ironically, the original meaning of the word "sin" is to miss the mark. *No one* does things perfectly every time.

This is *not* saying anything goes. The ability to articulate and enforce clear boundaries and standards is essential. Clearly communicated standards and methods for holding people accountable are basic building blocks of healthy groups and organizations.

In order to discuss effectiveness in addressing problems, we need to add assertiveness to our conversation. Assertiveness can be low or high. In combination with hostility and warmth there are four possible combinations: 1) When high hostility is combined with high assertiveness, it's expressed as *hot contempt*. In this style, people are intimidating, confronting, insulting, and working actively to undermine another person or get them fired. 2) When hostility is combined with low assertiveness the result is *cold contempt*. In work settings the two primary behaviors of cold contempt are a) avoiding others and b) backstabbing. 3) Warmth is combined with low assertiveness. I call this the *doormat* quadrant! In this style, the boss (or parent) abdicates his or her responsibility to lead or shape behavior.

None of these three approaches are effective! In the first two combinations the other party responds with defensiveness and negative reciprocity. In the third, they get away with murder—and others resent the supervisor or parent for not setting and enforcing healthy standards of behavior or performance.

The remaining combination consists of warmth in combination with high assertiveness. This option is *very* effective—and it's the style that people *use the least*! It's amazing to watch people gossip, stew, explode, rant, shame, stonewall, avoid, steam, lie, excuse, go numb, vent, roll over, use sarcasm, undermine, tease, pretend, retaliate, and suffer—reactions that take enormous physiological and emotional energy—rather than approach the problem with warmth and clear expectations. Asking for different behavior while treating a person with acceptance increases the odds we will maintain the relationship and work through the problem—together.

Addressing behavior that "misses the mark" in this manner has overwhelming advantages. Similar to the story of Rick in customized machines, when you give feedback with another party's interest at heart, they are tempted to listen and consider your input.

Attack and withdraw behaviors don't work because the whole personality is targeted, not just actions. *People don't change unless they feel accepted.*

As the following story shows, you can be warm even in situations that require dramatic corrective action.

Hard on the problem, soft on the people

When I met Mary Jo she managed a government subsidized, low-income apartment building—a tough job that requires tremendous skill. After she heard me talking about the potency of warmth combined with high standards, she told me the following story.

On the way to a meeting one morning she was walking through the county courthouse with an attorney. Coming toward them from the opposite direction was a middle-aged woman Mary Jo recognized. The two women embraced, talked enthusiastically, gave each other quick updates on their lives and families, expressed delight in seeing each other, and chatted for a few minutes before continuing on their separate ways. As Mary Jo and her colleague resumed their journey to the meeting, the attorney said, "That was neat. How do you know each other?"

"Oh," Mary Jo replied, "She was one of my former tenants. I had to evict her."

Mary Jo was a master at setting clear limits and enforcing consequences, *while maintaining a warm and caring relationship.* This allowed her to evict a tenant, yet retain their connection and avoid negative reciprocity. In Chapter Nine you'll learn several techniques that will help you master this valuable skill.

"All the managers are immature!"

The following is a true story about a time I was caught off-guard by the destructive behavior of a client, flooded, caught my error, backed up, and approached the problem more effectively. It's a good example of the power of thinking to change behavior and outcomes.

I conduct seminars and keynotes on this material titled the "Self-Defeating Habits of Otherwise Brilliant People." After a public seminar, a director from a large nonprofit agency in Rochester, Minnesota, approached me. Roxanne loved the class and asked me to come to her organization and conduct sessions for their managers. She said their organization was full of negativity and blame and could definitely benefit from my message.

On the first scheduled session at her organization, I was pleasantly surprised to see Roxanne sitting in the audience, ready to participate for the second time. "Wow, she must be a big fan of the material," I thought naively. "It must have made a big impact!"

In the few minutes before the presentation began people were chatting and enjoying coffee and rolls. A small group of managers sitting near the front of the room began discussing an organizational disaster that had occurred a year ago, which had delayed their paychecks for more than two weeks. (I later learned the error, which occurred right before Christmas and caused significant problems for most of their employees, originated in Roxanne's office.) Roxanne, who was sitting near the back of the room, overheard their private conversation. From across the entire room, she said loudly, "Are you *still* talking about that?! Do you know why this organization is so screwed up? Because all the managers in this agency are immature!"

The room became dead quiet. As the presenter, I was in an awkward spot. I didn't have the background information necessary to understand the underlying conflict, I didn't have permission from the key players to make this the focus of the day, and the agency hadn't hired me to resolve an active situation; I was there to facilitate a seminar. However, I didn't feel I could ignore Roxanne's comment.

I did my best to smooth over her statement and help alleviate the negative impact of her remarks, but when I left at the end of the day, I knew the group hadn't fully recovered from the sting of her accusation.

While I was on-site I stayed upbeat, but once I was "off stage" and on my way home, I found myself rerunning the "tape" of Roxanne's words. I thought, "What a jerk!" In an effort to justify my feelings of self-righteousness and anger, I went on a classic "search for stupidity."

It wasn't difficult to find facts to support my negative thinking. Despite the fact that Roxanne seemed to value my message about B.O., B.S., BIBS, flooding, and reciprocity, she started out the day by attacking everyone in the room—the very behaviors she had brought me in to alleviate!

Suddenly I remembered I had to do two more seminars at her agency. Aghhh! Maybe she'd be on vacation. I wanted to *avoid* her.

Then the arrow of blame turned inward. Maybe *I* was the problem! I hadn't exactly saved the day. Maybe I was a fraud, and I'm the one who should be serving fries! If I had been Nelson Mandela or Bishop Tutu, the situation would have been a piece of cake. Why hadn't I fixed it?

I was really on a roll. I felt angry and powerless, and I was starting to feel sick. The queasiness in my stomach shifted my attention. I wondered if I was getting the flu.

Oh thank heavens! I was just flooding! Once I realized that I was feeling miserable because of my inflammatory thinking, I knew I could alleviate my distress simply by changing my thinking.

Before I understood these principles, the thinking patterns of blame, self-criticism, and their accompanying physical reactions were daily experiences for me. However, for three years I had been practicing "baby in the back seat" and paying attention to my thinking. Now it was relatively easy to become *aware* of the change in my body chemistry and identify the cause.

I realized I was blaming Roxanne, because she had blamed the supervisors, because the supervisors had blamed her department. There were three Cycles of Contempt in one situation. I started my analysis over, dragging my thinking away from reflexive reactions, toward a more reflective problem-solving approach.

The thinking pattern that will save your sanity and productivity

In the reflective orientation we assume that others fall short not because of malice, but because there's a baby in the back seat, or because they lack skill, insight, or courage (self-confidence). Whenever I witness an act that seems callous or destructive, I ask myself, "Is this person lacking skill, insight, or courage?" When *I* make a mistake, I analyze it using the same set of questions. These six words—lack of skill, insight, or self-confidence—have saved me many hours of useless fuming and negativity.

Let's return to Roxanne's behavior. Might her actions reflect a *lack of skill*? Could she have accomplished her goal by talking to the group privately and saying something similar to, "Are you talking about the mistake Judy made last year in payroll? I know it caused hardship, but when managers keep circulating the story a year later, it reopens an old wound. We were coping with some very unusual circumstances, and it won't happen again. I'd appreciate it if you could let it rest in the past."

Roxanne didn't have that much skill and self-control—at least not that day, not in that moment.

How about *lack of self-confidence* or courage? Roxanne's group hadn't formally apologized to those affected by the error. The managers were still discussing the incident nearly a year later because they were still angry, and the extent of the snafu had not been acknowledged. Sometimes it takes tremendous courage to say, "I'm sorry," especially when others are harmed by our behaviors. At the time, Roxanne and Judy had withdrawn. They became defensive as a means of deflecting attention away from their department's behavior, hoping to avoid becoming the organization's next scapegoat.

Then I considered the possibility that Roxanne's behavior was the result of *lack of insight*. I don't think at any time Roxanne understood how deeply her outburst offended the managers or fully comprehended the steps necessary to put the incident to bed. Instead, she continued to feed the controversy by blaming and withdrawing.

Once I looked at her behavior with a less inflammatory eye, I was also able to look at my own behavior with more objectivity. I too lacked skill, insight, and courage in that moment. After her outburst, I literally did not know what to do. I had hit my growing edge and "missed the mark." That's what human beings do—over and over. If we receive warm, competent feedback about errors, we learn, and try again. If we make an error and the other person attacks, we reciprocate by retreating or countering his or her accusations.

After a few minutes of looking at the situation with different assumptions, I realized my nausea was gone. When I thought about returning to Roxanne's agency for the remaining presentations, I no longer felt a need to avoid her. I learned a visceral lesson that day about the power of the subtle choice we make every time we are frustrated. Do we search for stupidity? Or do we analyze the situation in a more reflective light?

I would suggest you have these six words tattooed on your hand: Lack of skill, insight, or courage. In lieu of that, at least memorize them. Use those half dozen words for the next few days every time you see someone behaving rudely, defensively, or destructively. See if you can't view their behavior as a lack of one of these three qualities. This practice will allow you to maintain a non-judgmental attitude toward them, and the absence of negative energy *will make you more effective.* Wire your brain to think of these words every time someone near you behaves inappropriately.

You can also use the same words to analyze your own behavior when *you* make an error. Rather than disparaging yourself for "being a bad person," "an idiot," or a "complete bungler," you'll find yourself analyzing how you could approach the situation with more skill, insight, or confidence. Once your thinking becomes more objective, your mood will lift, and you will be more motivated to change and more confident that improvement is possible. Self-induced bouts of depression will become a thing of the past, as will your need to escape them by targeting someone else.

In the next chapter you'll learn how to improve your problem-solving abilities even more, by using a powerful technique to open the dialogue with warmth and clarity—an approach that is loaded with benefits.

Chapter Nine

There Are Two Dogs
Inside of Every Man:
The One That Dominates
Is the One That's Fed

The ancient Chinese gave us this adage, and I often think of it when I'm working with individuals or teams bent on destroying other people's careers. When people behave defensively or aggressively, I know the other dog—the dog of empathy and cooperation—is lying in the wings, waiting. If I can put the distressed person at ease, reduce his or her fears, and identify a way to feed the dog that wants to be appreciated and connected, it emerges with relief.

People often avoid tackling tense issues head on because they fear they will make the situation worse. Negative past experiences have convinced them that direct communication is too risky, or that they lack the ability to navigate emotionally choppy seas. Rather than risk an explosive situation, which they fear they cannot handle, they resort to withdrawal, or backstabbing. However, in this chapter you will learn a potent, safe technique. You will never again have to sidestep an issue of importance at work or home. You can address tough issues, clear the air, and feed the dog of appreciation at the same time. It's a very powerful experience.

We'll go through an overview of the five steps and then you'll have a chance to sketch out a dialogue about a situation you'd like to improve.

1. Open the conversation in the energy of appreciation

Let's revisit three important pieces of information. John Gottman found that conversations end in the same energy they begin, 96 percent of the time. Harsh setups trigger harsh endings, and conversations that open in appreciation, almost always end in the same tone. Using biofeedback data, the HeartMath group found that when people feel and speak with appreciation their body rhythms become coherent, and they experience a synchronization of emotional, physical, and intellectual rhythms that allow them to perform at their best. In this physiological state, individuals are relaxed, clear, and receptive.

Think about the finding discussed in Chapter Two that feelings of shame, which are usually the result of an attack on the *person*, not a specific behavior, actually provoke more anger toward others and do little or nothing to bring about an improvement in behavior.

To be effective, in opening dialogue we will utilize the findings of these researchers: the power of warmth, calm, and avoiding shame.

The powerful, gentle dad

I watched my friend Bob Larrington demonstrate the power of appreciation perfectly. Bob farms with his family in South Dakota, and he was one of the best parents I ever had the pleasure of observing.

Many years ago he was out in the yard with his 7-year-old son, Tommy. Bob was seated on the tractor, anxious to get to his work in the field, while Tommy was running around the yard playing with the family dog. Bob glanced in Tommy's direction and gave him a warning about playing too closely to the auger, a dangerous, rotating conveyer belt that is used to move grain. Tommy paid no attention to his dad's instructions, as he was entirely focused on his playful pal. Bob stopped the tractor, climbed down, sat on the edge of the tiller and called his son over.

My heart froze. I adored Tommy, and he had disobeyed his dad. I expected Bob to yell at him, scold him harshly, or even shake him. Instead, Bob put Tommy gently on his lap, circled his arm around him protectively and asked, "Tommy, what did daddy tell you to do?"

I was mesmerized. I had never observed anyone parenting in such a loving, gentle fashion. I witnessed the two of them wrapped in this warm connection as Bob calmly explained the dangers of Tommy not listening to his dad. Bob had Tommy's total attention as Tommy melted into the curvature of his dad's powerful arms.

Bob could not have claimed this child's rapt attention if he had flooded. However, with a gentle approach, clearly based on Bob's love for his young son, the father was building a strong connection and thus *increasing* the possibility that Tommy would respond to his dad's concerns.

In the workplace, you can hardly sit down on the edge of the desk and invite a colleague to sit on your lap while you wrap them in a loving embrace! However, you *can* create a climate of relaxation and acceptance by starting with a positive statement of appreciation.

Remember, *people need to feel accepted before they will change.* As my friend and client, a vice president of IT (and a man with staggering intellect) said, "I became effective in dealing with other people after I realized I had the most impact when I was the least threatening."

Warmth dissolves a corporate stalemate

A project manager at a large construction firm, Fran, gave me this example of how appreciation can break through tension.

She and another project manager were in a meeting with two architects from an outside firm. The four of them were responsible for a joint project, but they had been unable to come to an agreement about a variety of complex issues. The meeting was not going well, and the tension between the two groups was increasing. Unexpectedly, the president of Fran's firm, Steve, dropped in. Fran was thrilled, and thought, "Steve will take charge of this meeting and put these architects in their place!"

However, Steve is a master of warmth and appreciation. He greeted the visiting architects with a smile and shook their hands. He gave them a sincere compliment on a building their firm had just completed for a university. As Steve praised their craftsmanship, Fran said she could feel the tension melt on both sides of the table. Steve expressed his delight in having great people on the team from both firms and that he couldn't wait to see their preliminary designs. He thanked them again, welcomed them to the company, shook hands, and left the room.

Fran said that the atmosphere in the room shifted from chilly frustration to warm relaxation. *Within minutes of his departure they were on their way to resolution.* Appreciation taps into the circuitry of the cortex where problems are solved.

This insight is priceless. When you open the dialogue, make your first statement a message that conveys your appreciation for *the relationship*. Note, I am not suggesting that you compliment the *person*. If you list two things that they do well and then move into a problematic area, they typically feel manipulated. Instead, express your desire to preserve your working relationship. If you didn't value the relationship and want to maintain it, you wouldn't be trying to fix the problem. *Put your commitment, desires, and investment into words.*

If you articulate sincerely how important someone is to you, the other person relaxes and is inclined to join you in fixing the problem. Fear or anger about the conversation will dissipate, and you will create an opportunity for joint collaboration.

With a child or family member you can say words similar to, "You're one of the really important people to me. I want to talk to you about what happened last night because when things aren't right between us, it troubles me throughout the day."

In the workplace you can say something similar to, "We work closely together, and it's important to me that we have a relationship based on honesty and trust. I'd like to talk with you about something that has the potential of getting in the way."

Or, "Unless the nursing department has a good working relationship with administration, we can't respond to clients efficiently. Would you help me with a problem that keeps throwing a monkey wrench into customer relations?"

The handshake that is used in almost all Western cultures evolved from a form of the appreciation ritual. When men were armed with swords, they would show their desire to talk peacefully by laying down their weapons. That ancient gesture evolved into the showing of an open palm, reciprocated and grasped by the other person.

In the first step of opening the dialogue, demonstrate that you have laid down your sword; you do not intend to blame, alienate, or shame the other party. Making a statement of appreciation conveys the message that you are there to preserve the relationship *and* you need their help in solving a problem that threatens it. Because we no longer carry swords, and since it is not appropriate to sit the other person on your lap, say what I used to tell my son when he was 3 years old and frustrated: "Use your words, Ben. Use your words."

2. State the facts

The ability to separate fact from interpretation is one of the most valuable skills in opening a problem-solving dialogue. *Facts* don't determine how you feel, your *interpretations and assumptions* do. In the 1960s, Albert Ellis clearly differentiated the flow between facts, our interpretations of those facts, and our emotions.

Ellis recognized that there's a split second after an event when interpretations and facts are mingled. If you are aware of this and can sort out the two steps, you will be very effective. This step takes practice because even *what* we pay attention to is shaped by what we deem important. For instance, a fashion designer might notice the blending of textiles and colors in people's clothing as they enter a crowded room; and a psychologist or dancer might tune into the body language.

Here's an example of how differing interpretations create differing emotions: Three people are walking down the hall at work and pass their boss, Emma, who is walking in the opposite direction. Although Emma is generally friendly, this particular morning she doesn't say good morning or make eye contact with anyone in the group.

Although three people witness the exact same event, there are at least three different interpretations. When Pat interprets ambiguous behavior he usually assumes the worst about others. He thinks, "Boy is she ever stuck-up. Since she got to be manager, her nose has certainly been up in the air!" As a consequence of his *thinking*, Pat will feel angry.

Linda's automatic interpretation is to blame herself. She thinks, "Wow, Emma must be mad! I shouldn't have disagreed with her in the staff meeting yesterday! Why can't I keep my mouth shut?" As a consequence of her thinking, Linda will feel anxious about their next interaction, assuming she will be reprimanded or treated with cold contempt.

Rhonda is aware that interpretations are tricky. The possibilities are endless. She's learned to think about the reasons people behave the way they do, rather than jump to assumptions about personality. Her reaction might be, "Gee, Emma acted like she didn't recognize us. I wonder if she has her contacts in." As a consequence of her thinking, Rhonda's emotional reaction would be negligible.

Although I've listed three interpretations of one simple behavior, there are obviously many more. Every time we interpret someone's behavior, we select from an infinite number of possibilities.

Opening the dialogue doesn't require that your assumption is correct. However, it is absolutely essential that when you make an interpretation, you know it is just that—speculation—not fact.

The wildcard of accurate interpretation: self-confidence

Ironically, self-confidence, which is really about our own state of mind, plays a significant role in how we interpret what other people are doing. You can see this in the following example. Imagine a young woman, Lora, enters a coffee shop after work to meet her coworkers. As she approaches the table, an attractive new employee, who just joined the company, gets up and leaves. If Lora feels *insecure* about herself, she might interpret his leaving as a sign that he wanted to avoid her.

If she feels *self-confident*, she'll assume he is leaving for a reason totally unrelated to her, and may even take advantage of his absence by sitting in his vacated chair.

Self-esteem is a filter. If we feel self-confident and worthy, we see others' actions in a neutral, or even positive, manner. When we feel lonely or unworthy, we view positive or neutral behavior as additional proof of our isolation.

Whether you're insecure about your attractiveness, your competency, ability to parent, cook, calculate, make friends, influence, reason, sell, motivate, coach, or speak, in situations where you feel insecure you will interpret behavior differently than in situations where you feel self-assured and competent.

The fidgeting boss

When people fail to differentiate between facts and interpretations, they often act on speculations as if they are real, and, as you know, they unwittingly play a role in bringing their fears to fruition.

Cole went in to see his boss, Mike, with a draft of a floor plan that Cole had volunteered to create. As Cole began to show Mike his work, Mike doodled, stared out the window, and checked his watch.

What could Mike's behavior mean? There are endless possibilities: Mike hates the plan, he's in pain and anxious about his doctor's meeting at 4:30 p.m., he just got bad news from home, he always doodles, he has to cut 10 percent of his staff including Cole, and so on. Unless Cole is aware that there are many possible interpretations, he will make a very common error and assume *his* interpretation correct, and act accordingly.

Cole, who often interprets behavior as rejection, believes Mike is doodling due to a lack of interest in his ideas. Cole rushes through his presentation and walks out of Mike's office muttering that he will never again volunteer. He tells his team that Mike is two-faced and doesn't give a hoot about employee input. He throws the plan on a shelf and when Mike asks about it later, Cole mutters that he can't remember where he put it.

Later, when Mike tries to follow up, Cole brushes him off, and Mike assumes Cole has lost interest. Mike draws the design without Cole's input, muttering about how little initiative employees show. When Cole sees that Mike has drafted a design without his input, Cole believes that his boss really didn't care about the team's ideas. The next time Mike asks for input from the team, no one volunteers. Mike concludes that he's tried to get the team involved, and his direct reports simply aren't interested.

Without questioning his interpretation, Cole never learns that Mike was distracted because just before their meeting Mike's director chewed him out about a report he had forgotten to complete. Mike's nervous preoccupation had nothing to do with his dislike or disapproval of the plan.

There is a simple solution. Cole could have checked his interpretation by stating factually and accurately his observations of Mike's behavior. Cole could say, "Mike, I've noticed you've glanced at your watch several times since I started my presentation."

If it's appropriate, use numbers. For instance, don't say to your teenage daughter, "You *never* put gas in the car!" Try, "Honey, the last two times I've gotten in the car after you've used it, it's been on a quarter tank or less." Avoid exaggeration—it will be seen as dishonest and manipulative. State your facts in such a way that the other party will agree with the accuracy and impartiality of your statement.

If the behavior is a pattern, with a history of failed promises, start with an accurate statement of that reality.

3. Ask the other party for help in understanding his or her behavior

In the past, I encouraged people to share their interpretations. For instance, Cole could say to his boss, "I think you're looking at your watch and doodling because you don't like my draft." However, it is more efficient just to say, "Can you help me understand why...?" This simple question short-circuits the guessing game, and leaves the door wide open for the other person to reveal his or her hidden "baby." Asking for help in understanding behavior is a respectful and neutral request for information, and is grounded in curiosity.

In general, individuals want to explain their rationale. Almost no one wants to be judged negatively by others. Even though I work with people who are often considered unpleasant by their peers and supervisors, *in two decades of conflict resolution work I've never gotten a hostile response from asking, "Can you help me understand why...."*

4. State the ideal behavior

This is a powerful and important step that people often overlook. When people are flooded or defensive, they state and restate facts and interpretations. They don't realize they *must* move to the future in order to solve the problem. Asking for what you want is like giving the other person a *golden thread* back into the relationship. You are stating what the other person or group can do to resolve the issue and restore the relationship.

Don't be afraid to state what you want, and the change you would like to see. It's not a demand. They can respond with their own request, or modify yours. Think of it as a starting point. Most people appreciate knowing what you want, especially if you've put your preferences in terms of specific behavior. Avoid global statements such as, "I wish you were considerate about time," and substitute something more exact, "I wish you would call me if you're going to be more than 10 minutes late."

For instance, after learning that Mike's focus was on other issues, Cole could have told Mike how he wanted to resolve the situation. He might have suggested, "Mike, I need your reactions to the floor plan design before the team moves ahead. Can we reschedule our meeting?"

Before you open the dialogue, spend time thinking about what you want from the other person. It might be as simple as setting aside time to talk, or a commitment to gather cross-functional data to work together on a problem. Don't make the mistake of the two men in the following story who argued for years without being specific about what they wanted.

The scruffy chemical dependency director

I was on a strategic planning retreat with the management team from a chemical dependency treatment center that I'll call "Sobriety Plus." Sobriety Plus developed coaching relationships with organizations. When a client suspected that an employee had a problem with alcohol or drug use, they utilized the resources of Sobriety Plus for assessment, referral, and if necessary, treatment.

While gathering background information before the retreat, I learned about a long-standing conflict. Paul, the polished marketing director and the person responsible for acquiring new corporate clients, had a long-standing conflict with his peer, Mack. Mack was the program director (and a recovering addict) who supervised the treatment groups and counselors. However, I hadn't been hired to facilitate their conflict. Our goal for the weekend was to rewrite their strategic plan.

Midway through our first morning together, this long-standing conflict erupted, and the two directors commenced to argue. The rest of the staff pulled away from the table, or turned in their chairs. Some of them walked out of the room to take phone calls or get coffee. They had heard it all before and once this conversation began, it took center stage for quite awhile.

I stood listening for several moments, unsure what to do. Was there a way to get them unstuck within a few minutes, or did I need to request that they table their discussion and stuff their emotions?

As I listened, I realized that they were stating and restating facts and interpretations. *Neither person was articulating what they wanted.*

I interjected, "What do the two of you want from each other?"

To my amazement, instead of ticking off a list of requests, they both fell silent. This argument had been simmering for two years, yet neither person had identified what they wanted from the other to resolve the issue!

Finally, Mack, the program director, said to Paul, the director of marketing, "You don't know anything about chemical dependency. You're out there selling our program and you don't know squat about addiction or how people recover."

I prompted him again, "Mack, tell Paul specifically what you want."

There was another pause, followed by a tentative, "I want you to go through the program as if you're a client. I want you to attend orientation and sit in on groups."

It was a pivotal moment. Everyone at the table froze.

Paul paused for a moment and then to my amazement he said, "Okay. Actually, I've wanted to sit in on group sessions, but I was afraid it'd be inappropriate."

I turned to Paul. "Paul, what do you want from Mack?"

There was another moment of silence. It stretched on—and on. Finally, Paul gathered up his courage to say what he had held back for two years, "God, man, get your hair cut! When I take you out on sales calls I'm embarrassed by how you look."

In his days of using drugs, Mack had hit bottom and remained there for a long stretch of time before he was able to maintain sobriety. Although he had been clean for many years, his days as an addict were reflected in his appearance. The clients that came to Sobriety Plus didn't care. They knew Mack had walked their walk and recovered. However, when Paul took him on sales calls to corporate HR offices, his wild hair and worn clothes were a definite liability.

Mack's reaction to Paul's request was a stunner.

"Sure. I would have done it a long time ago if you would have asked."

I have never forgotten that moment. When people don't ask for what they want, *they deny themselves, and the other party, the possibility of resolution.*

Don't let this happen with your important issues. Again, before you open the dialogue, identify the ideal behavior you want from the other person. Make it specific and make it positive.

5. State the consequence or open negotiations

You have just asked someone to alter his or her behavior. Are you willing to shift your behavior in return? For instance, Cole might say to his boss, "Why don't I check in later and we can reschedule our meeting. I'll call you tomorrow." Or the statement may be a negotiation, "If you can give me two minutes on this one detail, I can wait until later in the week for a more thorough discussion."

This statement can also be a *consequence* of what you will do if the other person doesn't change his or her behavior. If you are in a position of authority, your statement may be similar to, "If this happens again, I will move to a written warning."

In the situation of the daughter who brings back the car without gas, it may be, "If you continue to use the car without refilling the gas, it will be off limits for two weeks."

Starting out

The first time you use this approach I suggest you fill out the following outline *before* you have the conversation. It will give you time to sort out your thinking. You may want to open the dialogue with the situation on which you based your Cycle of Contempt.

Don't start with the worst problem in your life. Begin with more manageable situations. As your skill and confidence grows, you can tackle more sensitive concerns. At some point, talking in this manner will come to you naturally and you won't have to think about it ahead of time. This approach can become your best ally in maintaining relationships and resolving touchy issues.

Opening the dialogue

1. Affirm the relationship. *"I want to talk to you because...."* Tell the other party you value the relationship and want to preserve it.

2. State the facts. *"I noticed...."* State the facts accurately. Be specific and use numbers when appropriate.

3. Ask for help in understanding his or her behavior. *"Can you help me understand why...?"* Is there a hidden constraint of pressure? Is there a baby in the back seat?

4. State what you want. *"I'd prefer if you would...."* You cannot repair this relationship by focusing on the past. What do you want in the future? Describe the ideal behavior or result.

5. State what you are willing to do. *"I'm willing to...."* What are you willing to do to solve the problem? What is your part in reaching a solution? Are consequences possible? Be specific.

Practice what I preach: The unruly third shift

In my line of work I have used this five-step outline on hundreds of occasions. However, one time in particular stands out. I was teaching the "Self-Defeating Habits of Otherwise Brilliant People" seminar at a manu-facturing plant, when the operations director asked if I would facilitate a workshop for the third shift. We had accommodated the second shift during the day sessions, but the director wanted an offering at night for the last group. I groaned at the thought of delivering a workshop in the dead of the night, but the director's commitment to his third shift won me over, and we set a date. The director warned me that it was a tough group, and difficult to engage.

When I arrived at the facility it was past midnight. The workers who clamored into the room were young, disheveled, and dressed in T-shirts with graphics that one might see on Saturday night at a biker's bar. It was very clear that the supervisors cut this late shift group a lot of slack. We hadn't been together 30 seconds before I knew that they bonded through crude humor. As I started introducing the material, the off-color remarks continued to float through the air, but I pressed on, assuming that they would calm down and focus on the material.

After the first 20 minutes, however, the humor continued. I looked at the supervisors for help, but they were enjoying their normal late-night banter.

I thought about my options. I could get indignant and scold them. *Didn't they know how immature they looked?!* A scolding might stop their banter, but I would probably lose their cooperation and blunt any inter-est in learning. I could pull their supervisors aside, give them a short lecture on inappropriate behavior, and ask them to rein in their group.

Then I thought about analyzing their behavior by assuming it grew out of some lack of skill, insight, or courage. Maybe the third shift felt insecure about being in a classroom setting. Maybe some of this group was uncomfortable reading and writing. It wouldn't be the first time some-one had avoided work in a seminar because they couldn't read. Or maybe they simply didn't realize how uncomfortable I felt.

I decided to deal with the situation using an abbreviated version of the steps we just discussed: 1) a statement of appreciation, 2) facts, 4) what I wanted, and 5) what I was willing to do. I decided to delete the third step. In this setting asking, "Can you help me understand why...?" was opening a can of worms that would only take us further off task. I'd be satisfied if I could confront the issue in a respectful manner and ask for what I wanted.

A statement of appreciation (or in this case, an expression of goodwill):

"When Fred asked me to come and teach the third shift I agreed, because I didn't want you excluded from learning opportunities. I want you to have a chance to learn this material, because it will affect your lives in many positive ways."

Facts:

"I've noticed you're comfortable with a lot of rather crude humor. However, it's the middle of the night, I don't know any of you, and as far as I know, I'm the only woman in the building. I feel a little uneasy."

What I wanted:

"Would you be willing to stop your comments and focus on the information?"

What I'm willing to do:

"Then I will keep going and you can learn the techniques, which you may find surprisingly helpful."

I wasn't sure what they'd do. I had been pretty darn direct. This was a fairly blunt confrontation for a fairly large group of men who I barely knew—all this at 1 a.m.! Perhaps they would react to my request with humor, or make a crude comment ridiculing what I'd said. However, I was taken aback by what actually happened.

I went back to presenting the material and during the next three hours *no one* made another inappropriate comment. When I left, two of the men came up to me and said, "It's still dark out. If you'd like, we'll walk you to your car."

I was stunned. It was a wonderful experience of positive reciprocity. They had returned the respect with which I had treated them. On my way home, as the sun began to lighten the morning sky, I realized I had fed the other dog in this group of young men—and they had responded graciously.

Chapter Ten

You Can Be Effective *or* Self-Righteous—Pick One: Five Smart Reasons to Ditch Hostility and Blame

O n a fairly regular basis someone will ask me, "Well, I understand your point, Anna, but what if someone really *is* a jerk?" and proceed to tell me about a person who seems to operate outside the realm of rational behavior. Although their stories are often amusing, the storyteller usually admits that, realistically the "jerk" is a wounded, low-skill individual more deserving of compassion than contempt. Feeling chronically hostile and cynical is a miserable way to live. However, the question is fair and deserves a serious answer.

Is there ever a time when one should "give up" and conclude that the situation *is* totally the fault of the other person, it *is* permanent, and it *is* everything about them?

What about the "jerks" we interact with out of necessity? What's a useful way to think about the people who annoy us? Are "attack and avoid" behaviors ever justified, outside of a life-threatening situation?

Let's look at a political leader who faced this decision. This leader had plenty of reasons to treat another group with contempt. Regardless, he made a decision to sacrifice his "right" to retaliate, and he used the opportunity to be effective instead.

Retaliation or reconciliation: Nelson Mandela

Nelson Mandela, the former president of South Africa, wrestled with the question of effectiveness versus self-righteousness in an extreme and very public form. In his country, the white, Dutch government ruled with institutional racism, torture, rape, imprisonment, and the execution of thousands of black South Africans. If anyone had a reason to blame, Mandela did. Knowing this, the world watched in 1990 as he was released from prison, and later was elected president.

In his autobiography *Long Walk to Freedom*, Mandela tells how he was deeply influenced by the writings of Gandhi during the years he was incarcerated. He realized that blame and contempt, although "justified," would not move him closer to his goal of creating a healthy, viable government and society. Mandela focused on changing the system, not individuals or the white race. He suspected that if he created a more healthy system, it would feed the other dog and his country would heal.

Mandela wrote, "I know people expected me to harbor anger towards whites. But in prison, my anger towards the whites decreased and my hatred for the system grew."

Mandela let it be known that anyone who wanted to help rebuild South Africa as a nonracial democracy was welcome at the table. He broke a long-standing Cycle of Contempt, and reached out to white South Africans with an invitation to join him in solving their country's problems.

Together with Bishop Tutu and the former president, DeKirk, they created Truth and Reconciliation, a process that allowed individuals, white and black, to step forward and confess to political crimes in exchange for amnesty. Under the policy, both black and white citizens had a specific deadline to confess the crimes they committed under apartheid. If they refused to take accountability, they were liable for criminal prosecution.

It was a brilliant decision. It avoided a civil war. It allowed families on both sides of the conflict to receive reliable information about the fate of their loved ones. The process avoided hundreds, perhaps even thousands, of civil and criminal lawsuits—charges that would have taken decades to resolve. Truth and Reconciliation allowed people to admit wrongdoing, ask for amnesty and forgiveness, and rejoin the community with an opportunity to contribute to the rebuilding of their country. It replaced retaliation with a process for reconciliation and cleared the way for a viable future.

Videos of the tribunals were eventually broadcast in the United States and they were wrenchingly painful to watch as perpetrators on both sides of apartheid confessed. The stories were reminiscent of Zimbardo's prison experiments—in horrific systems, ordinary people commit heinous crimes.

However, many of Mandela, DeKirk, and Bishop Tutu's hopes were realized. Even though they were dealing with millions of people, they proved that healthy systems elicit healthy behavior *from the same people*. The country held its citizens accountable, but avoided exacerbating a costly power struggle. By retaining the skill base and knowledge of the previous administration, the newly elected government established itself with unusual speed. Whites and blacks united in unprecedented cooperation. A nonracial democracy was born.

Consequently, when people assure me that they know someone who *deserves* to be blamed, a person who qualifies as a *real* jerk, I respond only slightly tongue in cheek, "If you have more reason to treat someone like a jerk than Nelson Mandela does I'll grant you an exception. Make a choice between matching your adversary's tone and behavior, or moving toward your goal."

Everyday we make multiple choices every day between self-righteousness and effectiveness. Now you can make yours consciously.

The advantages of avoiding blame

1. **You'll dodge emotional-idiocy.** You won't make a fool of yourself screaming at colleagues, family members, or strangers who have a legitimate, although hidden, reason for their behaviors. An automatic habit of curiosity and concern will keep you in the problem-solving, rational center of the brain. Remember, John Gottman found that we can't hear what the other person is saying, even if we try, once we flood and our heartbeat rises above 100 beats per minute.

2. **Health and resiliency improve.** As covered in detail in Chapter Two, when you reduce the number of times you flood, you protect your body from the dangers of cardiovascular disease and the excess production of cortisol, a hormone associated with the inability to calm down, rapid aging, and damage to the cells that line the heart.

3. **Positive reciprocity accrues, and it matters.** For years you've been creating reciprocity with your words, tone, eye contact, and behavior.

What you've accrued is negative, indifferent, or positive. Because *you* are on the receiving end of the continual repayment of your own behavior, it makes sense to create positive reciprocity. Remember, despite what your parents said, you *are* the center of *your* universe!

In a study at Bell Labs, Robert Kelley and Janet Caplan sought out top-performing engineers as identified by peers and managers. It wasn't their intellectual IQ that made the difference. They had created positive reciprocity by cultivating relationships and friendships. When the top performers needed advice or input, their e-mails and phone calls were answered because their colleagues reciprocated their good will and concern.

4. **People will want you on their team.** Your ability to make progress toward goals, and bridge to other key players will solve problems and win friends. When you want to problem-solve with another party, the skills will be in your hip pocket. Using them can become as natural as indignation and flooding is for others.

5. **You'll earn a reputation as a trustworthy, can-do leader.** Because both Cycles of Contempt and Cycles of Courage are self-fulfilling, as individuals age, patterns become more automatic and less conscious.

The blame orientation, especially as it becomes automatic, will isolate you from others, and you will become more cynical, ignorant, and paranoid. You'll consistently be lured down dead-end roads of blame, mistrust, and negative cycles. Employees will unintentionally set you up to be suspicious of others if you tolerate their attempts to deflect personal responsibility through blame. You'll be buzzing around in a fog of adrenaline wondering why you're surrounded by idiots, and misunderstanding others' benign or even positive intentions.

In contrast, when your response to frustration consists of curiosity, concern, and compassion, you will develop a reputation as an effective, solid, trustworthy, and powerful problem-solver—the kind of person organization develop and promote.

As we age: Wisdom or ignorance?

All three assumptions—*it's your fault, it's my fault,* or *there's a reason*— self-validate. Imagine the impact over your lifetime as your experiences accrue. With reflective rather than reflexive thinking, you will become curious about people in all walks of life. You will learn about government, the stock market, hospital staffing, schools, highway maintenance, the newspaper, your neighbors, and other ethnic groups. You can find out why the highways are jammed, why the legislative process is slow, why the Palestinians and Israelis are mutually fearful. The understanding you gain will allow you to identify the best leverage points to fix whatever problems fascinate you.

When your automatic response to frustration is curiosity, concern, and the ability to open the dialogue, you will learn why your neighbor parks his boat next to the garage and not in it. You will discover why your brother stopped coming to family gatherings three years ago, and why your daughter doesn't want to play soccer anymore.

Instead of flooding you will be in the position to *learn* why the driver is digging in the back seat of her car, why your boss is suddenly closing her door, why the bride's father is smirking, and why the supervisor is missing from the floor.

At work you will be constantly gaining knowledge about the hidden influences in your organization. You will learn about its constraints, limitations, history, and assets. As you practice your skills you will gain confidence and insight. You will find yourself sharing what you've learned and educating others.

The people with whom you interact will trust you because you respect their efforts and are willing to learn about their constraints.

If you could compare my life 10 years ago with it now, you would see this difference with crystal clarity. All of these changes have occurred in my life through an increased understanding and application of the principles in this book.

In the past, blame and self-doubt were constant, unwanted companions that I didn't know how to dismiss. Now, like Bruce the Vietnam vet from Chapter Two, wherever I go, I can create and ride the energy of appreciation. Every frustration is an opportunity to learn, and every person, crabby or pleasant, has a wealth of hidden stories, experiences, and varying skills, but the same goal: the desire to feel valued and valuable, cherished and appreciated.

Love is stronger than terror because ultimately every impulse can be tracked back to our deep need for love.

—Deepak Chopra, M.D.,
Peace is the Way

Positive energy buffers frustration. You can use it consciously to grease the wheels of human interaction. It's good for your career, your relationships, and your heart. It shapes the quality of every interaction, every opportunity, and every challenge.

It's the best habit you can give yourself, your colleagues, direct reports, and loved ones.

Chapter Eleven

Creating Cultures of Appreciation: Respect, Pride, and Fiscal Responsibility

Do not wait for leaders; do it alone,
person to person.

—Mother Teresa

I was attending my fourth meeting with the executive team at a high-tech company. We were well on our way...addressing the underlying reasons for tension within the group. When I had first arrived at the company three weeks earlier, Hans, the CEO, told me that their executive meetings dragged on, hour after unproductive hour, punctuated by outbursts of hostility and blame.

Hans told me that people left the meeting with migraines and often team members would refuse to talk to each other for days after their gatherings.

We had made progress. This was our fourth meeting and we were proceeding in a civilized tone. However, when we adjourned for lunch I looked around the table and realized the executive team members looked pale and exhausted. I had taken away their source of energy—hostility—and I had not replaced it. The absence of anger and outrage left a vacuum. There was no passion, no connectedness.

When we gathered again in the conference room I changed the afternoon agenda. I shared what I had observed over lunch and explained that we needed to move further down the continuum—away from negative energy to solidly plant the group in positive interactions before we moved on. I leaned on my relationship with Hans, the CEO, and asked him to be the first "receiver."

I took out a blank piece of paper and said, "I'd like you to go around the table, and tell Hans one thing you respect about him as a person or one skill that he brings to this table that you appreciate." They stared at me as if I was mad.

I sat expectantly, without apology, as if I made this request every day and, of course, they would comply. "I'll write down your comments and give them to Hans. Then we'll move to the next person. If we spend 10 minutes on each person, we should be done in a little over an hour." They continued to stare at me.

I told the secret only I knew. "I *know* you respect each other and admire the commitment each of you has made to this company. Every one of you mentioned this to me during your interview. Now you need to tell each other. If we don't do this, the team won't have the energy it needs to optimize your work."

> *Lack of recognition is the number-one reason people leave their jobs.*
>
> —Randy Sigel
> "Seven Steps to Keep Top Performers"
> *Public Relations Journal* (February, 1999)

They realized I was serious. Greg, the VP of engineering, turned to Hans and thanked him for the tenacious dedication Hans had shown in his role as CEO. Greg commented on Hans's business and engineering savvy, and his ability to build rapport with customers. It was the first unadulterated statement of appreciation that had been made during a team meeting in more than a year.

They continued around the table. Each person made a statement about Hans's talents, perspectives, and commitment. I documented their re-marks, handed them to Hans, and we shifted to the next person. Each team member made a comment. Some said one or two things, and some spoke paragraphs of appreciation about each person. They expanded the assignment more than two hours. My hand cramped. I was delighted.

The energy shifted. Shoulders softened. It was the first time I saw them smile. They began building on each other's comments, and acknowledging how interdependent their achievements had been.

The tears that formed in the corners of eyes confirmed how much they had ached to hear exactly what they were now receiving. When we finished, everything had changed.

Resentments evaporated and transgressions were forgiven. Generosity and gratitude took center stage. It was as if someone switched stations from one of unrelenting criticism and accusations to a bandwidth of humility and compassion. These simple acts actually took tremendous courage—much more than when they raged.

For the first time I was certain that they would come through to the other side of their struggles. By creating an atmosphere of mutual respect they were being energized at a cellular level.

My job was more than half done. Within the energy of appreciation the systemic and process problems that had been the cause of their earlier hostility and hopelessness would be relatively easy to repair.

When organizations fail to make a commitment to positive energy, the daily grind of frustrations and delays and disappointments pulls teams and groups toward negativity, pettiness, and irritability. Without a conscious commitment to create positive energy, nothing compensates or rewards individuals for unnoticed investments and sacrifices.

Preserving goodwill

I consulted with a creative marketing firm in North Carolina that was struggling with tension. As my involvement with them drew to an end I challenged the group to adopt an appreciation ritual as a means of maintaining the positive energy they had created during our work together.

Since that time they've honored one of their team members at each of their weekly staff meetings. Each of the 14 employees name one trait their colleague brings to work that adds to their creativity, productivity, or atmosphere. Because the name of the individual is pulled at random at the meetings, the upcoming assignment shifts their focus during the week to *everyone*.

Their CEO, Mary Tribble, claims that this brief ritual not only transforms their meetings, it improves the atmosphere throughout the week.

Small acts of observation and verbal acknowledgement force the group to focus on their strengths and accomplishments. Without intentional, periodic, scheduled time dedicated to public appreciation, day-to-day irritants drain goodwill and energy.

> *Those individuals who lack the comfort of another*
> *human being may very well lack one of nature's most*
> *powerful antidotes to stress.*

—James Lynch, M.D., University of Maryland

Connections to others increase the enjoyment of positive moments and help us bear hard times. Researchers who studied the turbulent breakup of AT&T in the 1990s found that employees with supportive bosses experienced significantly better health than those with unsupportive bosses. Employees with aloof or critical supervisors had twice the number of illnesses, obesity, sexual problems, and episodes of depression as their more fortunate peers.

Even under the worst conditions—for example, combat duty in war—relationships make a difference in resiliency. A study of WWII veterans by the United Sates Office of the Surgeon General found that combat soldiers who were members of highly bonded, cohesive groups with strong identification had fewer psychiatric breakdowns in battle. Soldiers who were lonely and isolated suffered the greatest psychological damage.

World-class appreciation

Organizations that are deeply engaged in building and maintaining cultures of appreciation seem to do so effortlessly. When positive energy reaches a critical mass, it becomes infectious and self-replicating. However, I've never been in a highly positive culture that didn't consciously dedicate resources to recognizing and honoring employees, customers, and vendors.

When someone walks into Ryan Companies US, Inc., a national development, design-build construction and property management firm, you sense immediately this is an organization dedicated to its values. Symbols of meaning are everywhere.

Building lasting relationships
Ryan Companies US, Inc.

A photograph of the founding grandfather, James Henry Ryan, is displayed prominently on the wall. A full-size replica of the first Ryan service vehicle (a model "T") sits in the middle of the hallway. Meeting rooms are named for regional offices and are decorated with photos of projects their offices have completed. When staff visit the main office from outside the local area they feel welcome.

Ryan allows 5 percent of work time to be spent volunteering. Employees volunteer at local hospitals, soup kitchens, and social service programs. When a retired developer and customer had a stroke, employees took turns taking him to physical therapy.

People want to be cared about. When they know they are, they work their hearts out. You can't fake it. People know.

—Jim Ryan, CEO, Ryan Companies US, Inc.

Ryan employees form a tight-knit group that extends beyond the workday. A former Ryan project manager left the company for another firm and two years later he died suddenly. One of his former colleagues called his widow and asked how they could help. The following weekend a dozen employees went to the former employee's house and finished home-improvement projects, including pouring new concrete steps and painting the exterior of the house.

Every quarter, the company gathers for an all-employee meeting to discuss market changes, new projects, profit sharing, and stretch goals. The room is dead quiet, every employee from the CFO, to the CEO, mailroom and construction workers crowd into the room.

But the meeting starts with heart, not statistics. The first presenter on the agenda reports on volunteer projects. People who have benefited from Ryan volunteers also speak at these meetings as a way to thank employees and describe the difference they've made in the lives of others.

Recognition of employees is ongoing and the centerpiece of their celebrations. Every November, 700 Ryan employees begin peer nominations for the recipient of the James Henry Ryan Award for "Honesty and integrity in dealing with customers...," "Exceptional dedication and service...," "Keen loyalty and pride...," and "A willingness to assist and help others...." The CEO, Jim Ryan, and past recipients of the award review the peer nominations and Jim chooses one recipient.

The Ryan holiday party the following month includes current and retired employees from across the country, flown in at the company's expense. There's an undercurrent of suspense as the recipient of the James Henry Ryan Award is announced, and his or her spouse, children, parents, and siblings appear on stage. No one in the company, including the recipient, knows the award-winner except for family members, who are sworn to secrecy by Jim Ryan and his assistants.

The thought and sensitivity that goes into the event is represented by a $5,000 grant awarded to the winner. In keeping with company values, the award goes to the charity of the recipient's choice. Other employees share the joy of the recipient's opportunity to benefit others. This company knows how to build positive energy.

Best practices

Much has been written on acknowledging and recognizing employees. Although these books are rich in ideas, you can also learn from your own experiences. When have *you* felt truly honored and appreciated at work? When did you feel that recognition programs were superficial, or even insulting? What were the ingredients? What made it special and meaningful, or hollow?

Seek input from employees. This can be collected in focus groups, interviews, or surveys. If you create a standing group that is committed to this subject, include upper management and rotate the positions every year. That way you'll get fresh ideas from a cross section of the organization and more people will take ownership in the process.

Create or open channels of internal and external customer feedback. Encourage employees to interview between three to five key customers a year to learn how their work affects others and what the ingredients of satisfaction are from the customer's perspective.

Benchmark other companies. I'm always asking my clients to tell me about moments when they've felt honored or truly appreciated at work. Following are a collection of recent answers.

1. After attending a seminar on this material a customer service group started an "Anti-flooding" team to identify and eliminate sources of frustration and aggravation.

2. A client in Alaska told me about a memorable time when his management team became targets for a pie-throwing contest to help boost spirits during a period of particularly painful constrictions.

3. Some organizations create monthly newsletters or postings on a central board that celebrate staff accomplishments. Again, this is a constant reminder to be alert to the contributions, competence, and sacrifices of individuals and groups.

4. A social service client hosts an annual reward event that celebrates people in a humorous and eclectic ways, such as "rookie of the year." They give coupons for coffee, books, or movies that can be awarded on the spot for "going the extra mile."

5. A client that was under tremendous pressure broke up the monotony of the afternoon production quotas by spinning a huge, wooden, homemade wheel every day at 2 p.m. The prizes, which were imaginative and harebrained, averaged around $10. However, they were awarded on a random basis and everyone on the floor was eligible. It provided a few minutes of cheer, joking, chatter, and stimulation. They took pride in the homemade wheel and the hands-on, amateurish charm of the awards.

6. The CEO of Murphy Warehouse in Minneapolis sends a handwritten birthday card to every employee. While I was working there, I heard about this practice spontaneously from at least 10 different employees. Murphy also has a practice of granting loans to long-term employees. The human resource person told me no on has ever reneged on a loan.

7. Murphy also allows employees to donate vacation or sick time to employees during a crisis. When an employee suffered a stroke a year from retirement, employees voluntarily paid his health and pension contributions for a full year so the employee could retire with a full pension.

8. In one high-appreciation culture in England, the managing director (CEO) excused himself from a conversation with a member of Parliament to open the hallway door for the janitor who

was carrying a cumbersome box. The incident had occurred years before I arrived. However, his behavior made a lasting impression. During two days of consulting I heard the story from four employees.

9   A client told me about a practice that meant a lot to employees. They have three call centers and only one of them offers 24-hour service. When the 24-hour location is closed for maintenance, the overnight calls are routed to another site. Folks at the receiving locations aren't thrilled about having to work overnight, so they make a party out of it. The manager brings in espresso machines and makes lattes and mochas throughout the night, and takes a moment to visit with each of the 200 employees and thank them as he delivers a drink to their desks.

10. One memorable client, Bev, told me defiantly that she not only initialed her shipments, as required by management, she signed her whole name! She created her own unique strategy for finding pride in her daily work. Employees who are able to affiliate with their successes and resolve their own errors quickly develop a heightened sense of ownership and pride. As Bev puts it, "When I screw up, my boss pats me on the back while he pounds me into the pavement. We're a cool team."

These practices are fun to read. However, the best rituals of appreciation will be unique to the culture and nature of your organization. Rituals are meaningful when they are consistent with the values and identity of the organization and tap a deep desire for connection and the experience of being human within the privilege of a community.

Staying in touch

At the end of the book you will find information on audio versions of this material, mini-posters, and "train the trainer" opportunities. There is contact information for keynotes, skill-building seminars, and monthly e-mails to reinforce what you have read and strengthen your skill set.

For the sake of your workplace, health, family, and world take these ideas to heart. Feed the right dog—the dog of respect and appreciation—in yourself and others. Remember reciprocity. Be hard on the problem but soft on people. Love is good.

Appendix

Transforming the Enemy

Our desires shape the data our brains generate. If we decide some-one is a jerk, our brains cooperate and filter out facts that disagree with our prejudice. We selectively filter memories and perceptions that support our beliefs about someone, or something, even if we believe we are reviewing *all* of the pertinent details.

Thomas Kuhn concluded in *The Nature of Scientific Revolution* that even scientists don't "see" data that are inconsistent with current beliefs about their field of study. Max Planck, a physicist, wrote, "A new scientific truth does not triumph by convincing its opponents and making them see the light, but rather because its opponents eventually die and a new generation grows up that is familiar with it."

If scientists, who base their work on precision and objectivity, struggle with "seeing" data under their microscopes or at the end of their telescopes, imagine how easy it is for laypeople to convince themselves that what we *want* to believe is true.

The following story is a dramatic example of how my unconscious choice to "search for stupidity" rather than "search for a reason" shaped my opinions about another person (and thus I became part of the problem).

Although this story is from my personal life, the lessons I learned have profoundly shaped my work.

"Searching for stupidity" versus "searching for reasons"

During the second week of my new job at the Department of Education in South Dakota, I noticed a woman standing demurely in the corner of an elevator. She had striking, blond hair falling to her waist, and a gaping hole in her sweater.

I was amused by the contrast of her natural beauty and the glaring flaw in her clothes. A few weeks later colleagues introduced us, and we discovered a mutual love of books, music, and conversation. As I got to know her, I realized that her choice of clothing reflected her personality quite well. Jenny was brilliant, attractive, and rebellious. There was always a button missing, a hem slightly undone, or sleeves that hung below her wrists.

South Dakota, with its low population and scarce amenities, is a "do-it-yourself" state. If you don't create your own entertainment, you're not very well entertained. Hence, after Jenny and I met, we quickly became wonderful, fun-loving friends who cooked up all kinds of interesting forms of things to do, such as watching the moonrise by the river, midnight swims, and winter picnics amidst that state's untamed beauty.

Years later Jenny moved to Wisconsin to continue her training as a nurse practitioner and I returned to Minnesota to enter graduate school. Despite our physical distance we stayed connected through phone calls and intermittent visits.

Soon her calls included breathy, excited updates on Stan, the new man in her life. Despite an intense attraction at the onset of their relationship, by the third year of their relationship, Jenny began to vacillate between happiness and despair. Periods of intimacy were punctuated with estrangement and tears. After one of their painful breakups, Jenny called me with a sobering announcement, "I'm pregnant."

My heart sank. Missing from her life was the financial stability and emotional foundation a new mother and infant needed. I felt powerless to help.

Stan and Jenny made one last attempt to reconcile after the discovery of Jenny's pregnancy, but their reconciliation lasted only a few weeks, and they broke up for the last time. Jenny, with her endearing qualities of pride and defiance, was determined to raise her child alone. Several months later, she home-birthed a beautiful, healthy daughter, Alicia.

During the months that followed, Jenny and her close-knit circle of friends struggled with grief for the missing father. I prayed that Stan would re-enter her life, or Jenny would find a partner who would lovingly raise Alicia as a daughter. However, the years passed, Alicia grew into a precocious youngster, and we continue to hear nothing from Stan. The magical stepfather never materialized.

Through mutual friends we learned that Stan had moved across the state and married a woman with two children. Although he was aware of Alicia's birth and had returned to visit his parents in the town where Alicia lived, he never stopped to see his daughter. His behavior seemed irresponsible and incredibly callous.

When Alicia was present, Jenny and I stayed matter-of-fact about Stan's absence. But privately, our dislike for him became a source of passionate camaraderie. Our anger, like all contempt, had a subtle pay-off. No matter what strains developed in the relationship between Jenny and I, there was always a handy source of agreement—we could instantly connect and be energized by focusing on our mutual dislike of Alicia's father.

However, when Alicia turned 7 she began reacting to Stan's absence. She cried herself to sleep and become increasingly preoccupied with her absent father. She was restless and agitated at school. It was obvious that she needed to connect with her father, or find closure to the possibility that he might return.

During one of my visits to Wisconsin, Jenny got a babysitter for Alicia and the exhausted mother and I went out for a quiet meal. The conversation turned to the well-worn subject of Stan's absence. However, with Alicia's unhappiness weighing heavily on my mind, something shifted, and a sense of discomfort grew in my heart. I began listening to our conversation with a *detached* perspective and realized that our images of Stan were distorted by contempt.

Jenny and I described the problem as if the whole problem were Stan's fault, as if everything about him was useless, and he couldn't change. In reality, I wasn't behaving well either. Jenny and I were using our creative denigration of Stan as a familiar source of bonding. I was beginning to see that my behavior was also part of the problem. By working so hard to be loyal to my precious friend, I had unintentionally made Alicia's struggle more difficult.

In that moment I realized Alicia wasn't suffering just because of her father's behavior, she was paying a price for mine too. The cost of my self-righteousness contributed to our inability to solve the problem.

I put down my fork, surprised by what I was about to say. "Jenny, we have to stop talking about Stan as if he's the enemy. We have to reach out to him. He needs to know how important he is to Alicia."

There was dead silence. Jenny looked as if she was struggling to understand what I had just said. "We need to go find him and tell him how important he is. We have to at least try."

I knew I had taken a risk—siding with Jenny about Stan's irresponsible behavior was a familiar ritual of our friendship. But suddenly I realized that by not reaching out to Stan, Alicia was paying a price.

Jenny was taken aback by my sudden unwillingness to view Stan as a hopeless deadbeat. Eventually, her desire to ease her daughter's pain would trump her anger.

Jenny hesitated. "Let me think about it."

The next day, during a long drive back to Minnesota, I had hours to mull over what had happened. I realized that the power of my anger had kept me from seeing Stan in a reasonable light. Because of my disappointment in his behavior, I wanted to dislike him. I had unconsciously given my brain the command, "Search for stupidity! Stan is a jerk!" and my brain had responded. I swept over the complex story of their relationship with a brush of contempt. I finally realized that the allure of self-righteousness indignation also boxed us in, leaving no possibility of resolution.

During the drive I decided to try a mental exercise. I was determined to come up with as many answers as I could to the question, "Why *would* a person do what Stan had done? What would cause a *reasonable* person to withdraw?"

I gave my brain a totally different command, "Help me understand." I analyzed the situation using reflective, problem-solving questions.

What was Stan's "baby in the back seat"? Could he think Alicia was better off without him? Maybe he felt awkward and didn't know *how* to initiate a connection after all these years. Perhaps when Stan discovered Jenny was pregnant he asked her to put the child up for adoption and she had refused. Perhaps, overwhelmed with anger and fear, she had told him to stay away.

Maybe he felt inadequate and ashamed, and thought Alicia wanted him to stay away. Perhaps he was ill. Possibly his new wife was putting pressure on him to leave his daughter in the shadows. Maybe he thought his lack of involvement would make it more likely that Jenny would find a partner.

Then something hit me suddenly. I realized that when Jenny got pregnant she had been teaching birth control at a local clinic. Maybe Stan didn't want to be a father at that juncture and felt the pregnancy had been intentional. Perhaps he felt justified in his withdrawal and lack of support. Maybe he felt trapped and responded by refusing to take responsibility.

I realized these thoughts were speculations, but even *contemplating* them was breathtaking. I had been hoodwinked by my own thinking! When I wanted to see Stan as the "bad guy," I overlooked important facts and my mind created an image of him that fit my intention to make him the scapegoat.

When I examined the situation without blame, and tried to *understand* him, my hostility toward him dissolved and I saw the facts in a totally different light. I even considered facts that I had previously ignored. Similar to scientists, blinded by the limitations of their existing paradigm, my mind limited the data to support my intentions.

I still wanted Stan to take responsibility for his daughter, but now, without the baggage of contempt, I could think of a multitude of reasons for why he might have withdrawn. As well, I saw an endless number of ways to reach out to him and invite him into Alicia's life.

Several days later Jenny called and read me the letter she had written to the absentee father. She had written poignantly about Alicia's longing for him. She prepared a small package and included recent photos of Alicia and stories she had written at school.

Jenny and I edited the letter over the phone, until all that remained was a plea for his presence in her life. During that critical conversation we cried, laughed, and supported each other in the importance, and strangeness, of this new direction.

Stan responded. Strained phone calls between Stan and Jenny eventually evolved into plans for a meeting. Several weeks later, Jenny, Alicia, Stan, my son, Ben, and I sat down for Thanksgiving dinner in my home.

Jenny and I were dizzy with the reality that he was really there. It had been seven years. We couldn't believe it was happening.

Alicia sized her dad up and down and vacillated between, "Isn't he cool?" and "Can we go now?" That evening she began a cycle of emotions that ran through happy, sad, mad, happy, and would take several years to run its course.

Despite all of our wasted negative speculation about Alicia's father, there he was, looking older, a bit fragile, with a slight tremor in his fingers and a hesitation in his voice. But bless him—he was there.

Alicia is now a beautiful 16-year-old. Her father has remained an active, loving presence in her life, and recently volunteered to help Alicia with her upcoming college expenses.

I learned a lot from that experience and have often reflected on the power of my thinking to create my reality.

I suspect that other people are caught in the same bind of filtering, judgment, distorted perceptions, and self-fulfilling behaviors.

In many ways the experience with Alicia's father laid the foundation of my work.

- ▷ When we tap the energy of contempt, we turn a hurting, insecure person into an enemy: we sever relationships and lose the possibility of resolution.
- ▷ If I want to believe that someone is a fool, my mind will make it so.
- ▷ If I want to *understand* why a person is behaving in a particular manner, different data becomes available.
- ▷ Self-righteous indignation makes it *more* likely, not less, that the other person will behave in irresponsible ways.
- ▷ Being hard on the problem, but soft on the people appeals to the good in people and increases the chances of success.
- ▷ Being needed matters to people.
- ▷ Holding others accountable in a climate of warmth is infinitely more effective than silence and denigration.
- ▷ One person can take the first step that breaks a cycle of contempt.
- ▷ It is never too late.

Index

About the Author

ANNA MARAVELAS is internationally known for her ability to transform negative cultures into climates of respect, fiscal responsibility, and pride.

For 20 years she's resolved conflict and restored trust in organizations. She has a graduate degree in psychology with advanced training in system thinking and conflict resolution.

As president of TheraRising.com (St. Paul, Minnesota) she delivers keynotes and seminars in the United States and abroad.

About thera rising

Thera (Greek): To heal

Tools to deepen and sustain your learning

Anna delivers keynotes, seminars, and trains trainers on the material in this book under the title:"The Self-Defeating Habits of Otherwise Brilliant People."

Also available:

Print material and CDs
Consulting and Teambuilding
Free monthly e-letter with stories, research and anecdotes

For information go to www.TheraRising.com
Or contact Anna at info@TheraRising.com